A Word For Us

by

John C. Fuller

Well of Wisdom Publishing House
Los Angeles, CA USA 91506
www.wellofwisdompublishing.com
info@wellofwisdompublishing.com

A Word For Us
Copyright 2022 © John C. Fuller.

Published by Well of Wisdom Publishing House 4/1/2022

ISBN # (Paper Back): 978-1-7370927-2-8
ISBN # (eBook): 978-1-7370927-3-5

Library of Congress Control Number: 2021924007

A Word For Us

by

John C. Fuller

Day 1
GOD'S POWER ACTIVATED

"Three different times I begged the Lord to take it away.
Each time He said, "My grace is all you need.
My power works best in weakness."
So now I am glad to boast about my weaknesses, so that
the power of Christ can work through me. That's why I take
pleasure in my weaknesses, and in the insults, hardships,
persecutions, and troubles that I suffer for Christ. For when
I am weak, then I am strong."
2 Corinthians 12:8-10 NLT

Passage of the Day: 2 Corinthians 12:1-10 and James 4:3.

In 2 Corinthians 12:8-10, Paul references a "thorn in his flesh" —an area of weakness in his life. Desiring to escape the pain and discomfort of this weakness, Paul called on the Lord for help and asked God to remove this area of weakness completely. Paul's desperate cry for deliverance makes me think of the thorns in my own life. We all have areas of weakness or brokenness in our lives, but instead of following the example of Paul by facing those areas, we pretend they don't exist, and everything is okay in our lives. Furthermore, instead of recognizing and investigating our own thorns, we often find ourselves pointing out the weaknesses we see in others.

We don't boast about our weaknesses because pride prohibits us from doing so. Society has also placed such a negative connotation on the word *"weak,"* we are too ashamed to admit when we have weaknesses. As a result, we suffer in silence, wear smiles on our faces, but deep down inside; we need help.

James 4:3 teaches us that we do not have because we do not ask God. So if we are too ashamed to *admit* we are weak and need help, how can God truly help us? In our scripture reading for the day, we see that Paul refused to ignore his area of weakness. Paul went to God for help, and what was created to break him turned him into a prayer warrior. Change and transformation are always within our reach through prayer, but we have to exercise our faith and call on God for help.

In life, we can face many different thorns. Some of us face relational thorns, like constant family drama. Some of us have trouble discovering or completing the assignment God has called us to complete during our time here on Earth. Similar to Paul's experience, I believe God will not remove these areas of pain, brokenness, or weakness from our lives; instead, He will teach us how to live with them victoriously. We can't change our families, but God can teach us how to love them. We can't change the calling assigned to our lives, but God can teach us how to walk in our callings. No matter the situation or circumstance, we should exercise our faith and activate God's power in our lives by asking Him to guide and direct us. Paul taught us that if we continue to call on God's name —He will answer us because God desires to help us in the big and little details of our lives.

God's power is activated in our lives when we call on His great name. God's grace is sufficient, and His power is made perfect in weakness! It's okay to be weak and ask for help. We find help and strength when we call on the name of Jesus. There is power and healing in the name of Jesus. Be proud of the weaknesses, hardships, or troubles you may face. God will make a way and bring you out ten times stronger. God will intervene on our behalf in every situation. For when we are weak, through His might and Spirit, we are strong!

PRAYER: Heavenly Father, thank You that Your power works best in my weakness. In Jesus' name. Amen

Reflection

ACTION STEP: Make a list of your weaknesses, and ask God to give you strength and direction in these areas. Ask Him to show you how to be strong where you are weak.

Day 2

PRAISE BEFORE THE BLESSING

How long, O Lord, must I call for help?
But you do not listen!
"Violence is everywhere!"
I cry, but you do not come to save.
Must I forever see these evil deeds?
Why must I watch all this misery? Wherever I look,
I see destruction and violence.
I am surrounded by people who love to argue and fight."

"Even though the fig trees have no blossoms, and there are
no grapes on the vines; even though the olive crop fails, and
the fields lie empty and barren; even though the flocks die in
the fields, and the cattle barns are empty, yet I will rejoice in
the Lord! I will be joyful in the God of my salvation!"
Habakkuk 3:17-18 NLT

Passage of the Day: Habakkuk 1:2-3, Habakkuk 3:17-18,
Psalm 30:5, and 1 Peter 5:10.

Yesterday, we discussed addressing the weak areas of our lives by calling on God for help. Today, we will explore addressing the pains we have experienced in life. Have you been honest with God about the pains you've experienced in your life? Have you shared with Him how you believe those hardships affected you, changed you, or hurt you?

Take a moment to think about the afflictions, persecutions, trials, and tribulations you have faced in life. After your moment of reflection, take a moment and thank God! Thank God for the wisdom and strength you gained from the betrayal, heartbreak, or disappointment. Thank God that He did not allow the hardships you faced in life to break you. Thank God for keeping you throughout the years and for making it this far in your journey. Now, thank God for all the blessings on the way!

Psalm 30:5 teaches us that the tough times in life last for only a moment, and joy will soon overtake our lives. 1 Peter 5:10 promises us that God will restore all that we thought we lost after suffering a while, and He will make us strong in the process. Therefore, praise God for the joy that cometh in the morning. Praise God for what is and what is to come. Praise God in the midst of every storm you face in life because His word promises that after the rain clears, we will see the Son. God is with you in the storm, and He will renew your strength as you wait upon Him! Let God hear your praise before you see His victory! All you need is one word, and that one word is "Hallelujah." Give God your highest praise. Your breakthrough is on the way. Stay prayed up and praise God in advance!

PRAYER: Heavenly Father, I just want to say thank You for keeping me throughout the years, and thank you for the blessings that are the way!

Reflection

ACTION STEP: Take a moment to pray and simply thank God for all He has done for you over the years of your life. List some of the blessings you have experienced after the storms you faced in your life.

Day 3
WHAT ARE YOU THINKING?

"But now, since you didn't believe what I said, you will be silent and unable to speak until the child is born. For my words will certainly be fulfilled at the proper time."
Luke 1:20 NLT

Passage of the Day: Luke 1:5-23 and Proverbs 23:7.

The birth of John the Baptist is foretold in the first chapter of the Gospel of Luke. To summarize it - an angel (Gabriel) appears before Zechariah (John's father) to relay a divine message from the Lord. Zechariah's wife (Elizabeth) will soon be with child and give birth to a son, who will be named John. Due to Zechariah and Elizabeth's old age, Zechariah doesn't believe the word delivered by the messenger of the Lord. In response to Zechariah's unbelief, Gabriel shuts his mouth, and he will remain silent until the child is born. Often in life, we experience the same unbelief. God plans to do something great in our lives, but the way we think and the words we speak can get in the way of what God wants to do for and through us.

There are many reasons why we struggle to accept the promises God has spoken over our lives. One area our unbelief can stem from is our struggles with toxic thoughts. Our thoughts have the power to limit God's ability to move in our lives. Proverbs 23:7 states, as a man thinketh, so is he. What we think about ourselves and God often shapes the words spoken out of our mouths.

Our inner thoughts have the power to shape our behaviors as well. Toxic thoughts can often lead us to act or behave in ways that hinder the betterment of our lives. I often struggle with overthinking, indecisiveness, and being overly critical of myself in my own life. This has caused me sometimes to doubt what I know God has promised He will do in my life. Furthermore, my negative thoughts and lack of faith in what God promised sometimes caused me to steer from the path of right living and into a life of sin.

Zechariah was a religious man. When the angel Gabriel appeared before him to deliver God's message, Zechariah was in a sanctuary performing his religious duties, but had his religion become a habit? Had he lost faith in the God he was praying to? When the angel approached Zechariah, he told him, *"Zechariah, your prayer has been heard."* Zechariah was praying for a blessing but rejected the blessing when God answered him. Some of us have developed a habit of prayer, but if we look beyond the surface, do we lack the faith that is supposed to accompany prayer? We may tell God what we want but do we believe God will actually answer our prayers? Some of us even speak to God but don't have the faith to believe He will talk back.

Remember that without faith, it is impossible to please God. God cares about our actions - what we do, but He also cares more about what we think - our thoughts. Do you have faith that God will do what you ask? He's not asking for big faith, just faith the size of a mustard seed. Then watch God take our baby faith and do mighty things with it.

PRAYER: Dear God, help me to increase my faith. Amen

Reflection

ACTION STEP: What are some of the toxic thoughts you struggle with, and how do they impact your faith? What are you listening to or watching that causes these toxic thoughts? Once you figure out what that is, give it up for 21 days and document the difference in your thought patterns.

Day 4
GOD IS WITH US

"All right then, the Lord himself will give you the sign.
Look! The virgin will conceive a child! She will give birth to
a son and will call him Immanuel
(which means 'God is with us')."
Isaiah 7:14 NLT

Passage of the Day: Isaiah 7:14, Matthew 1:18-24, and Deuteronomy 31:6.

One of the names given to Jesus before His birth and through the words of the prophets was Emmanuel, which means God is with us. God is with us all the time. He's there right now as you read these words, and He's with us throughout every moment of our day. God wants to be seen. He wants to be known. He wants to walk with us, talk with us, and wants to be our Friend in the midnight hour. The midnight hour represents the darkest hour of the night, and spiritually it represents the dark or hard times in our lives.

When I am awakened in the middle of the night or when I have trouble sleeping, I often wonder if someone was thinking of me and if that was the reason I couldn't sleep. You may experience this as well. Randomly waking up in the middle of the night and struggling to get back to sleep, or unexplained struggles with insomnia. During those moments, I learned that someone was thinking of me and trying to get my attention. That Someone was God. I learned that we are often awakened in the middle of the night because God is trying to get our attention and wants to talk to us.

He can't get our attention during the busyness of our days, so He calls for our attention in the quiet moments at night. I've also learned that some of the dark and hard times in our lives were designed to get our attention and pull our focus back to God.

During the dark or difficult times in life, you may feel alone or troubled and desperately begin to seek God. You may wonder where God is in the midst of the chaos or if He even sees you, not because you're doubting God, you're simply looking for more. You're looking for more than just another sermon or a lecture. You're looking for a God encounter, to hear from God and be reassured that God did not abandon you. Stop at that moment and remember to trust God! He promised never to leave nor forsake us (Deuteronomy 31:6). So we are never alone. The God who made us is the God who is with us —even in the midnight hour. Through all the troubles we face and, in the battles, we are fighting —God is standing with us —fighting those battles while holding our hand. Cancel the negative report you were going to share with others because God is behind the scenes working it all out for our greater good. And remember, when you have God as a friend, you don't need to worry about an enemy. There may be people that don't like you, but they can't stop you. There may laugh at you, but they can't overlook you. God being for us is more than who is against us!

When you can't sleep at night, wake up randomly in the middle of the night, or are experiencing a dark time in life —turn your focus to God and have a conversation with Him. Use those moments to connect with God and develop a closer relationship with Him.

PRAYER: God, thank you for being with me at all times! Amen

Reflection

ACTION STEP: How can you spend more time with God today?

Ex: Say an extra prayer, read your Bible, worship.

Day 5
TAKING RESPONSIBILITY

"When Joseph woke up, he did as the angel of the Lord commanded and took Mary as his wife."
Matthew 1:24 NLT

Passage of the Day: Matthew 1:18-25.

Have you ever had to take responsibility for something that wasn't yours? One of our greatest examples of a man who did this with tremendous grace was Joseph, Jesus' father. When Mary was chosen to be the mother of Jesus, I'm sure God took her husband into account — the man who would help nurture, develop, teach, and groom Jesus. But we often don't consider how this impacted Joseph. I'm sure it wasn't easy covering Jesus and Mary while also dealing with the whispers that Jesus was conceived before Joseph and Mary were married. Or dealing with the truth that he wasn't actually Jesus' father. I'm sure it wasn't easy navigating the constant threats against Jesus' life —constantly moving his family from city to city to protect Jesus while also being a present husband and father to his other children. However, throughout the scriptures, we never hear that Joseph complained or refused to fulfill God's assignment on his life. Joseph simply obeyed everything God told him to do. He was committed to serving the Son of God and covered and protected Jesus as his own.

Like Joseph, when God calls us to walk alongside others, our job is to obey God. Our job is to listen to God and not our feelings. When we are assigned to cover or walk with someone during the seasons of their life when God is still developing them, we may begin to question God about our new responsibility. We may even question if we are truly equipped to handle the responsibility. Maybe the individual is not the best person to be around, or maybe being in their life causes you to deal with the inconveniences of their baggage. It could even be how you feel when you're around them. They may have a bad vibe or have hurt you in the past. No matter the circumstance, having this person in your life is a struggle for you, and you constantly find yourself asking God why you have to remain in a relationship with them. I want to offer a new perspective. Maybe it's not about who they are now. Maybe God has you in their life to support who they will be in the future. God could be calling you to help this person become who God wants them to be. Maybe God wants to use your influence to develop them for the future He has for them. You may think you have all the facts about this person, but is it possible that you have come to the wrong conclusion?

In life, we must learn to become more understanding and loving towards one another. We must learn to truly practice loving our neighbors as we love ourselves. Remember that you too may have some of those same flaws or qualities, and there are people God has assigned to your life to help you. Give people room and grace to grow into who God has called them to be, even when it's hard. I'm not saying to become best friends with the people God has assigned you to cover, mentor or lead, and I am not saying the relationship will be a lifelong one.

Maybe God wants you to help them this one time and then keep it moving. I am saying take into consideration that everything happens for a reason and follow God's instructions. Trust God and have faith that if He calls you to the relationship, He will give you the grace to walk in it. We become more Godlike when we take responsibility for what is not ours (see John 21:15-17).

PRAYER: Heavenly Father, help me not neglect those I am assigned to. Help me to love them as you have so loved me. Amen.

Reflection

ACTION STEP: Who are you currently assigned to that you may have neglected? If you are not assigned to anyone, think of other ways you can be a blessing unto others?

Day 6
JESUS IS ENOUGH

"Then a cloud overshadowed them, and a voice from the cloud said, "This is my dearly loved Son. Listen to him.""
Mark 9:7 NLT

Passage of the Day: Mark 9:2-8.

In today's message, I wanted to remind you that Jesus is enough. Within the Christian community, we often focus on theology and scriptures but forget about the importance of knowing Jesus and having an intimate relationship with Him. Knowing scriptures, reading the word, and understanding the Bible are all important to our growth and spiritual health as believers, but we shouldn't just stop there. We also place a lot of focus on what others say about Jesus and their experiences with Him. However, we should pay more attention to what Christ says about Himself and who He is to us. God is still speaking today, and He can speak directly to our hearts. If we could get to Jesus, He is enough!

God promises the best to His children in every area of our lives, and He did not create us to settle for less. He doesn't want us to settle in life, and He doesn't want us to settle in our relationship with Him. Don't settle for anything less than God. Earthly structures like churches can be here today and gone tomorrow, but God and His word will remain forever. Church leaders may change, but God is here forever. Relationships come and go, but Jesus came to stay. Jesus is always present and never changing.

He loves us when we are unlovable. He walks with us, talks with us, and remains present when nobody else is there. Above all, our relationship with Jesus should be the primary focus of our lives. And His love and companionship are more than enough.

Recently, one of my best friends reminded me that we don't always have to be in a church to have church. We can have church anywhere as long as Jesus is present because Jesus is enough. When you don't know which way to go in life, remember Jesus is our Driver! When we need a miracle, remember we have access to the Miracle Worker Himself! When we find ourselves at the end of our rope with nothing left to give, Jesus will be there. Some people won't go the distance with you but, Jesus will go the entire way. Jesus is enough no matter what we face in life.

PRAYER: Jesus, thank you for being enough! Amen

Reflection

ACTION STEP: Write down everything you already know about God.

Day 7
HEARING WHAT JESUS IS SAYING

*"Jesus said to the people who believed in him,
"You are truly my disciples if you
remain faithful to my teachings.
And you will know the truth, and the truth will set you free."
John 8:31-32 NLT*

Passage of the Day: John 8:31-32.

Are you hearing what Jesus is saying?

Often in life, we get caught up in believing or feeling like we can handle every situation thrown our way on our own. However, when we do things our way and choose not to follow the directions God has given us, we can end up at the wrong destination or in a situation God never intended for us. I have struggled with this at times because I can be quite impatient. Through trial and error and the wisdom I have gained along the way, I have learned that when I am presented with a problem, the first thing I need to do is step back, pray and talk to God about what is going on. Sometimes, God answers in the moment, or it takes some time, and He responds to me in another way. I've learned to look for God's voice all around me. For example, He sometimes communicates with us through our conversations with other people.

In addition, we may not understand or neglect to follow what God is telling us because we have not been set free from the hidden struggles holding us back in life. Hidden struggles, like past hurts or unresolved pain, can cause us to struggle to hear God or properly interpret what God is saying to us. We experience true freedom when we discover and accept the truth about God and ourselves. Finding true peace in our lives requires discovering and accepting truth, no matter how hard that truth is to receive. Accepting truth leads to peace within ourselves, and peace within leads us to have more of a humble heart. Those ingredients —accepted truth, internal peace, and a humble heart —help us to hear God a lot more clearer and allow us to follow His instructions with ease.

Today, I pray that you are filled with joy, happiness, love, compassion, patience, forgiving hearts, and peace in your life!

Now take some time to hear what Jesus is saying to you.

———————————

PRAYER: God, help me hear more of You and less of me. Amen.

Reflection

ACTION STEP: Would you consider yourself impatient? As a result of impatience, what have you taken into your own hands instead of waiting on God?

Day 8
FRIENDS

"There are "friends" who destroy each other,
but a real friend sticks closer than a brother."
Proverbs 18:24 NLT

Passage of the Day: Proverbs 18:24.

Friends, how many of us have them?

There will be seasons in our lives when we'll require support outside of ourselves. This support should come from a nonjudgmental place. A safe place where we can pour out our hearts before people who genuinely love and support us. A place where we find encouragement and rest after being overwhelmed with the many challenges we face in life. This safe place in our community, and that includes our friends.

When choosing our support systems and friendships, we should first identify what a friend is. Friends are people in our inner circle. Friends get a different level of access into the inner workings of our lives, our expectations for them are higher, and the investment in the relationship is greater. A friend is also someone who will hold you accountable, but they do not hold you hostage. Read that again. When choosing friendships, we must also use wisdom. We should ask God to show us the difference between accountability and jealousy or hate. When we think about support in our friendships, we generally think of support during difficult times in life. Yes, God blesses us with friends who support us through the difficult seasons in our lives, but our friends are also there to support us with our blessings. Therefore, we need genuine support from people who will help us navigate our blessings and not speak negatively against them. We must practice caution because we may encounter someone with an unhealthy heart whose hate can be mistaken for accountability. Furthermore, without proper support, even our success can overwhelm us and sink us.

We must also learn to decipher between a friend and an associate. Friends are people in our inner circle, and associates represent those people in the outer circle of our lives. Their access is limited, our expectations for these relationships are lower when compared to friends, and the investment in the relationship is less as well. An associate can also be defined as someone who isn't evil enough to be an enemy, but they are also not safe enough to be a friend. We must learn to discern who is a friend and who is an associate. Then, it's our responsibility to make sure the people who mean the most to us don't get the least of us.

As we mature and continue to grow in life, it is also important to pause and take time to inventory and evaluate our friendships and relationships. Sometimes we don't have the wrong people in our lives or on our team; we simply have them in the wrong positions. And when we have them in the wrong position, we often find ourselves expecting something from someone they can't deliver. We can give someone the title of a close friend, but that doesn't mean they have the capacity to be one. We find ourselves constantly nursing hurt feelings and unmet expectations when this happens. No matter how much we try, we cannot pull something out of someone God simply did not put in them. And maybe they are a great friend to someone else, but they simply don't have the capacity to be a great friend to you.

To avoid these frustrations and failed expectations, we must evaluate our friendships and relationships in every season of our lives. We must ensure that everyone is in the correct position, or if they even qualify for a position. That person may have produced friendship fruit last season, but that doesn't automatically mean they will in the next season. As you reevaluate your friendships and relationships, don't see it or take it as a moment to be judgmental or critical towards others. See it as a routine health check for your life and wellbeing. View it from a place of personal growth and self-evaluation. These aren't bad people; you are simply adjusting bad relational placement decisions.

The reevaluation of friendships is very important to our personal growth. We can't become new people without new influences. Your environment plays a significant role in who you are as a person now and who you become in the future. That environment can include friends, family, associates, co-workers, neighborhood companions, and more. Hanging around positive and new influences can be extremely beneficial to our growth.

In the same way, that hanging around old friends and relationships that have expired can become extremely detrimental to our lives and personal growth. Being around the wrong people can block our blessings, and we have to decide whether we would rather remain stagnant to please others or change for ourselves. Unhealthy environments and relationships can also interfere with our ability to hear God properly. Sometimes, we can't receive the clarity we've been praying for in our lives because we're unknowingly committed to remaining in our current situation or environment. Comfort blocks clarity, and to receive a vision for the future; we must welcome God's divine disruption into our lives.

Remember, God didn't create us to settle in life, which means He didn't create us to be complacent in our relationships either.

God did not create us to live life without support. God created us for community, but finding and creating the right community is key.

PRAYER: God, bless me with wisdom and discernment to properly evaluate the placements, friendships, and relationships in my life.

Reflection

ACTION STEP: Evaluate the relationships in your life.

Day 9

ARE YOU WEARY?

*"Then Jesus said, "Come to me, all of you who are weary
and carry heavy burdens,
and I will give you rest. Take my yoke upon you.
Let me teach you, because I am humble and gentle at heart,
and you will find rest for your souls. For my yoke is easy to
bear, and the burden I give you is light."
Matthew 11:28-30 NLT*

Passage of the Day: John 8:31-32 and Hebrews 12:1.

There are many burdens we can carry in this life —worry, stress, financial troubles, anger, jealousy, disappointment, insecurities, pain, the opinions of others, grudges, or pro-crastination… just to name a few. There has to come a time in our lives when we decide, it's time to stop carrying these burdens and give them over to God. If not, choosing to carry these burdens will eventually weigh us down and can cause us to travel down a path of destruction in life. In Matthew 11, Jesus promised healing for our hearts and rest for our souls, but the only way we receive this healing and rest is to make a trade —give our burdens to Him and receive our promised rest. Sometimes it's hard to let go. Sometimes we struggle to release even the bad things we have experienced in life. But remember, God always does what's best for us. We can rest assured that God will never leave our sides, He will strengthen us throughout the process, and in the end, every situation will work out for our good.

Hebrews 12:1 states, "...let us strip off every weight that slows us down, especially the *sin* that so easily trips us up." Sin is another heavy burden that weighs us down in life. Sin can be defined as disobedience to God or God's word. Sin breaks our connection with God, and we can't be right with ourselves or God until we are born again and receive forgiveness for our past, present, and future sins. As human beings, we have all been born of the flesh, but have you been born again —born in the Spirit? We know when we were born (when and where), but do we know when we were awakened spiritually? In life, we can follow a high moral standard but still lack the forgiveness we need for our sins. All our good deeds — reciting Bible verses, praying every night, and staying out of trouble aren't enough for the forgiveness of our sins. Through Jesus, we find rest from life's heavy burdens, and through Christ, we also receive salvation and forgiveness from the burden and penalties of our sins. We need to be born again. When we are born again, we are renewed on the inside. That internal renewal then changes everything on the outside.

Hebrews 12:1, also states *"...And let us run with perseverance the race marked out for us."* Are you running your race? God blessed each of us with gifts, and it's up to us to use our gifts to fulfill and serve our purposes here on Earth. Comparison, envy, and jealousy are also heavy burdens that weigh us down on our walks in life. However, Hebrews encourages us to focus on the race specifically marked out for us. It is important that we focus on our own races and not try to run someone else's. The same Jesus saves us, but our lives have different assignments and requirements.

Your blessings will also look different from those around you. You may be standing in need of prayer, but God may answer your prayer differently from others. You may be praying for a breakthrough, but your breakthrough may take longer than your neighbor's. We keep from stumbling by focusing on our races.

As you reflect on today's message, ask God to show you what He needs you to do. When we give God what He wants when He wants, He will provide us with what we need. If you are weary and need God's help in an area, keep praying for help in that area. God wants us to be shameless and persistent in our prayers. Some of us are shameless and persistent when sliding in someone's DMs or applying for jobs nonstop on websites like Indeed. You can do the same with your prayers. I pray that you have a great and blessed day. I pray that you find rest from your weariness. I pray that you begin to have conversations with God about your race and purpose in life. I pray that God blesses you with a humble heart to follow His instructions and serve out His will. For what is in His will is His way, and we should follow!

PRAYER: God, help me give you more of what You want rather than what I want. Amen

Reflection

ACTION STEP: Reflect on the following questions:
Are you carrying any burdens?
Have you been born again?
Are you running your race?

Day 10

GIFTED

"We have different gifts, according to the grace given to each of us..."
Romans 12:6 NIV

Passage of the Day: Romans 12:6-8.

How are you currently using your time?
Some of us may be dedicating our time and energy to useless things when we consider the bigger picture God has for our lives. We may find ourselves tired or overwhelmed because we are doing too much while also doing all the wrong things. Sometimes, we may even blame others for our irresponsible use of time or for wasting our time. How often do we actually look inwardly and check ourselves for wasting the time God gave us? Instead of acknowledging our shortcomings, we also complain about the gift of time God has given us. *"I don't have enough time in the day"* or *"If I could just have an extra day during the week, I could get the items on my to-do list completed."* Today, I want to challenge us to ask God to teach us how to wisely use the time He has given us.

Everyone has a gift given to them by God, and it is up to us to use those gifts to serve our purposes here on Earth during the time we are given. Time moves quite fast, and life is too short to be complacent. Don't be afraid to ask God what He wants from you or what is your life's purpose. As human beings, we know everything that is good for us —the best foods to eat and the best skincare products for our skin type. But how many of us know what we are good for? Do you know your purpose? Do you know what you are living for? Have you decided what your life will speak in the end? Start using your time and energy to discover the answers to those questions. Start using your time and energy for the things God intended, and slowly you will notice that your life moves away from being weary, tired, or overwhelmed. The rest, peace, and joy you've been searching for God has the yolk for it. God carries the weight of the world on His shoulders, and He never intended for us to carry the weight of our lives on our shoulders. God makes time to walk with us, talk with us and hold our hands through everything. However, we enter this place of ease with God when we live our lives according to His design and original plan for our lives. And when you're walking in His will and purpose for your life, and it still feels like God isn't there for you or moving in your life —continue to keep your faith and trust in Him. No matter what it looks like, we must remember that when God shows up, He shows out! Your time is coming.

PRAYER: God, what is it that You need and want of me at this moment?

Reflection

ACTION STEP: What can you do differently today to ensure you are using God's time wisely?

Day 11
THE THIEF

"The thief's purpose is to steal and kill and destroy.
My purpose is to give them a rich and satisfying life".
John 10:10 NLT

Passage of the Day: John 10:10, John 14:1-6, and John 14:12-14.

Recently at church, a reverend called up all the children in the sanctuary to the front of the congregation and and spoke a very profound word of encouragement to them. His message was directed towards the children, but I found the message profound for all believers of the faith.

His message stemmed from a familiar cartoon series, "The Looney Tunes." You may be familiar with the coyote and roadrunner from the Looney Tunes franchise. Suppose you are not familiar with the series. In that case, the storyline of each episode generally focuses on Wile E. Coyote, who develops countless unsuccessful plots and schemes to catch, kill and eat the Road Runner. The coyote is relentless in his pursuit and tries everything in his power to destroy the roadrunner, but his death traps never work. In our own lives, imagine that the coyote represents a thief. A thief can be defined as anyone or anything keeping us from having a relationship with Jesus Christ. A thief wants to kill who God created us to be, steal our inheritances as children of God, and destroy the purposes God assigned to each of our lives. The thief also comes to take everything valuable that God placed inside us.

You may wonder, *"what do I possess that's valuable."* The thief is after our purpose, strength, courage, wisdom, compassion, and so much more. However, like the coyote, the thief tries to destroy our lives, but he always fails.

When the thief comes and attacks the different areas of our lives, have you noticed how God always provides a way of escape and the circumstances always work out in our favor? Psalm 91:1-4 states, *"Whoever dwells in the shelter of the Most High will rest in the shadow of the Almighty. I will say of the Lord, "He is my refuge and my fortress, my God, in whom I trust. Surely, He will save me from the fowler's snare and from the deadly pestilence. He will cover me with His feathers, and under His wings I will find refuge...."* When we have a relationship with Jesus Christ, we will always escape the assaults, attacks, and pressures of the enemy. The enemy wants to destroy our lives, but Jesus died for us to live a glorious life and life more abundantly. Jesus wants us to do more, love more, serve more, and live out our dreams. Christ never promised that this journey would be easy, but He did promise we would experience overwhelming victories because of His love for us (Romans 8:37).

If the coyote represents the enemy.
With Jesus, we are the invincible road runner.

———————————

PRAYER: Jesus, thank You for helping me escape the enemy's attacks!

Reflection

ACTION STEP: How can you love more, serve more, and live out your dreams?

Day 12
DAILY BREAD

*"Be careful to obey all the commands I am giving you today.
Then you will live and multiply, and you will enter and occupy
the land the Lord swore to give your ancestors. Remember
how the Lord your God led you through the wilderness for
these forty years, humbling you and testing you to prove your
character, and to find out whether or not you would obey His
commands. Yes, He humbled you by letting you go hungry
and then feeding you with manna, a food previously unknown
to you and your ancestors. He did it to teach you that people
do not live by bread alone; rather, we live by every word that
comes from the mouth of the Lord."*
Deuteronomy 8:1-3 NLT

Passage of the Day: Deuteronomy 8:1-3, John 6:26-27, and
John 6:47-58.

The term *"bread"* has many different meanings. We
use the term to refer to something we eat, and in some
cultures, it's a colloquialism for money. When we consider
bread from a natural perspective —the bread we eat or the
financial resources we acquire in life —how often do these
"breads" actually leave us satisfied? Do these forms of bread
have the ability to meet all our needs in life? Yes, financial
blessings solve our financial burdens and woes. But there are
many wealthy and financially successful people in the world
who will testify to the fact that money can't buy us the things
that really matter in life —like family, love, joy, and peace.

The bread we consume for nutritional purposes temporarily calms our hunger, but the natural human experience proves we'll soon be hungry again. These facts point to one truth —man cannot live on bread alone.

In the Christian faith, Jesus is referred to as the *Bread of Life*. Jesus Christ is the living bread, and He is the only form of bread that can truly satisfy us. He is the only form of bread that can bring us sustainable fulfillment, joy, peace, strength, and everything else in life we are relentlessly searching for. When we choose to receive this Living Bread, we choose to live by, stand on and have faith in every word that comes from The Lord.

We've all heard the saying, *"you are what you eat."* If that statement is true naturally, what does it mean for us spiritually? When we live by the word of God, we experience the fullness of life here on earth. However, if we consume the wrong forms of spiritual bread, we'll often find ourselves spiritually malnourished, weak, and vulnerable to the attacks of the enemy. Sometimes, we become picky spiritual eaters, picking and choosing which portions of the Word we want to receive and consume and picky about what we want to hear from God.

For others, the bread God supplies also becomes like manna —perfect during its intended time and a burden once it has run its season. Every now and then, God fills a need or gives us a seasonal word that we hold onto far beyond its season. As a result, something that was once a blessing becomes a burden in our lives (see Exodus 16:20).Yes, God can supply our bread and many other things, but none of that should replace God and the new bread He wants to bring in our lives. We sometimes want to stay where God has us, but we limit God because we have no idea where God can take us.

Yes, God can supply our bread and many other things, but none of that should replace God and the new bread He wants to bring in our lives. We sometimes want to stay where God has us, but we limit God because we have no idea where God can take us. Some people would rather rest in the place of a repeated blessing versus trusting God to receive a fresh and better blessing. But isn't God meant to be our *daily bread*? Doesn't the word of God promise, we will experience new mercies *every morning*?

God is a provider, and He will supply everything we need in its proper time. But we must remember, we need God more than we need something from God. In life, the things we want aren't always what we need. And when we find ourselves constantly chasing worldly desires or ungodly desires of the heart, those desires can lead us down paths of destruction and sorrow, especially when we desire those blessings more than we desire God. God should be our greatest heart's desire (see Matthew 6:33). God promises that He will do exceedingly abundantly more, above all that we could ever ask or think. He simply wants us to hold on to His hand, have faith in His power, and accept the Bread of Life as our sufficient daily living bread. He's all we truly need.

PRAYER: Jesus, thank You for being the living bread.

Reflection

ACTION STEP: What are you currently chasing in life? Is this something God has instructed you to pursue, or is it something that you want?

Day 13
FRUITFUL BRANCHES

"Yes, I am the vine; you are the branches.
Those who remain in me, and I in them, will produce much fruit.
For apart from me you can do nothing."
John 15:5 NLT

Passage of the Day: John 15:1-8.

Does your branch produce fruit?

God is the Gardener; Jesus is the Vine, and we are the branches. Our purposes in life were designed to flow out of our connection to God, and God always intended for us to be branches on earth that produce purposeful fruit. The Bible also states that the key to living a fruitful life is abiding in Christ. There are many ways we abide in Christ, but today I want to discuss three —reading the Bible, continuously praying, and being resilient in the face of life's many storms.

When we allow the word of God to abide in our hearts, our chances of abiding in Christ increase. The word that is in you comes out of you, and knowing the promises and instructions of God as recorded in the Bible is one way we begin to produce fruit in our lives (see Joshua 1:8). God explains the Bible, and the Bible explains God. Once we learn to appreciate and study the Bible, we'll learn more about who God is.However, a lack of knowledge can deter us from knowing who God is, who we are, and who we belong to. Don't be afraid to pick up your Bible to learn more.

If you want a piece of heaven here on earth, get a piece of the word in your heart!

We also remain connected to the Father when we stay in a posture of prayer. God's Word teaches us who God is, and it also teaches us the right way to pray. Many of us were taught to pray in the name of Jesus, but how many of us were taught to pray for God's will in our lives. In Matthew Chapter 6, the disciples ask Jesus to teach them how to pray, and Jesus responds by teaching them what we now know as the Lord's prayer. One of the lines in that prayer says: *"Thy Kingdom come, Thy will be done in earth, as it is in heaven (v.10)."* Through this one scripture, Jesus taught us to pray for the Lord's will in our lives, and that was just one specific method of prayer. Throughout the scriptures, we are given various prayer strategies, and those strategies ensure that we pray prayers that unlock God's plan, will, and promises for our lives. The Bible is our phone book, and prayer is our telephone. We have to make sure our calls and messages reach our intended receiver.

Lastly, we live fruitful lives when we stay close to Jesus. I want to encourage you to stick with Jesus through the tough times in life. With all the chaos and confusion in the world today, I believe God is trying to tell us something —it's time that the children of God start walking in their purposes. We were all put on this earth to utilize the gifts God has given us, and those gifts were designed to support our purposes in life. Each day, we should be doing something that serves our purpose, but that may be difficult at times.Life comes with many unexpected trials and hardships that subsequently reveal our imperfections. However, I believe some of those imperfections were designed to help us master our God-given gifts. Romans 8:28 teaches us that all things work together for the good of those who love God and are called according to His *purpose*. The next time you face a storm in life, instead of running to people, places, or things for an escape —run to the Father. Ask Him to show you the purpose of the storm and how He wants you to use it to be fruitful in purpose. Through the good, bad, happy, and sad times. Stick with Jesus Christ, our true ride or die!

The Bible also states that our branch is pruned or cut to produce more fruit. God wants us to live rich and full lives, and when we do what God asks, He will give us what He has promised —a fruitful life.

If you ever need a reminder of why you should stick with Jesus or abide in Him — read John 15:1-8.

PRAYER: God, thank you for being the Gardener who helps me produce more fruit.

Reflection

ACTION STEP: How can you produce more fruit from your branch?

Day 14
THE UPGRADE

"A host always serves the best wine first," he said.
"Then, when everyone has had a lot to drink,
he brings out the less expensive wine.
But you have kept the best until now!"
John 2:10 NLT

Passage of the Day: John 2:1-12.

In John 2:1-12, Jesus and His disciples are attending a wedding celebration. When the wedding hosts run out of wine, Jesus' mother comes to Him and asks Him to address the wine shortage. Jesus reluctantly agrees to His mother's request and turns jars filled with water into wine. After the guest at the wedding begin to drink the wine Jesus miraculously produces, the master of ceremony pulls the groom aside and enthusiastically proclaims, "You have saved the best for last!" We've all heard the saying, *"why settle for less?"* but what happens when we decide to settle on more?

In life, we sometimes crave more. When we lack something in life, we sometimes revert to wanting more. For instance, more money, more friends, or more time. We often think more means better, but how many of us have experienced *more* that has left us unsatisfied? For example, maybe God wants you to wait on Him for a better job instead of taking that promotion or working those extra hours to make more money.Or maybe you're considering going back to some old hangouts to rekindle some old friendships.

But God wants you to heal more, so He can bring you better friends who support the new person He is developing you into. A small group of new friends who will truly be closer to you than a brother. Whatever we lose or give up, God can replace it, remake it or improve it. Trust Him. Or maybe you desire more time in each day, but God wants you to learn better time management skills and how to better manage the time He has given you. God did not create us to be stagnant, and more of a bad thing is simply more of a bad thing. Some of us spend our lives searching for more, but our search for more can cause us to miss out on what's better. God doesn't just want us to have more in life, He wants us to have the best in life, and His best is always better.

Some of us are also tempted to settle for what appears to be *more* than we have right now because God didn't show up when we expected. But God's delay does not mean denial, and our blessings do not show up in our lives according to our desired timetable. God is an on time God, and He doesn't make mistakes. When He shows up, He shows out and will bless us with better. Hold on to faith and believe God will provide you with something even better than what you were praying for.

For God to bless us with better, we also have to invite Him into our lives. Jesus will show up wherever He is invited and welcomed. Jesus' invitation to the wedding was the first step into everyone in attendance witnessing His power and glory. But for Him to perform a miracle, a problem had to present itself. When we open the door to Christ and accept Him into our lives, we must also understand that there willbe tests and trials we have to face as followers of God. It may appear that the Lord is knocking you down, but time will show He was simply developing you to raise you up.

The Bible teaches us that God humbles the proud, but He also exalts the humbled (see Matthew 23:12). Sometimes, the trials we face in life are meant to humble us, but in the midst of our trials and tribulations, God remains by our side. We serve a just, fair, and balanced God. He rebukes us, and He also blesses us. When we humble ourselves before the Lord and follow His instructions or commands, He promises to bless us and upgrade our lives.

I want to encourage you to stand firm, confident, and keep a smile on your face as you trust God through your current circumstances. Don't settle for less and don't settle for more —settle on receiving God's best for your life. Stay in a posture of contentment, and God will do the rest. Remember that God saves the best for last, and every season of life takes us higher and higher. Everything new things that God does for us will be better than the last thing He did for us.

PRAYER: Heavenly Father, thank You for where I am in my life today. I may have plans for my life, but you determine my steps. Help me be open and receptive to receiving better rather than settling for more. Help me to have a humble heart, so I can continue to follow Your instructions for my life. Also, give me the strength and patience to wait on Your best. In Jesus' name, I pray, Amen.

Reflection

ACTION STEP: What are you currently craving more of?

Day 15
IT'S NOT YOU, IT'S ME

"God replied to Moses, "I Am Who I Am.
Say this to the people of Israel: I Am has sent me to you."
Exodus 3:14 NLT

Passage of the Day: Exodus 3:4-14 and Matthew 7:24-27.

T here will come a time in your life when you'll have to tell someone, *"it's not you, it's me."* Have you ever experienced a time in life when you've started to change and couldn't explain to others what was happening because you didn't fully understand what was happening yourself? Your priorities start to change, the music you once loved doesn't excite you anymore, and your attention has shifted to things you believe are much better or more important for your life. Maybe you're in a season where you're not connecting with old friends like you used to, and you've decided to focus on building something within yourself that cannot be broken. Those around you may have a hard time accepting this but don't you for a second start second-guessing your decisions or the new season God is ushering you into. Don't take these changes as something negative. You will soon realize the ground you're standing on is shifting, and as the ground around you continues to shift, you will soon transition over to standing onto Holy ground.

The funny thing is before this change becomes evident, you'll realize you've been sensing it for years. You've been standing on Holy ground all this time, but you've been too afraid to take off your shoes and step into this new moment. When the foundations of our lives begin to change and everything we built our lives on no longer make sense, that is a scary reality to accept. But an even scarier reality is not stepping into the new and forfeiting everything God has for you. Therefore, you have to shake every piece of dirt and dust off your feet and step into this Holy moment. Step into the new and away from all the burdens or troubles from the past and anything else hindering your growth.

Through my personal life experiences and history with God, I have found that God uses our seasons of uprooting to show us who we are. God often shakes up the ground of our lives to awaken us to a new dimension of who we are, so we can finally figure out who we are at our cores. Sometimes, we do not know who we truly are until we are placed in a situation where the greatest version of ourselves has no choice but to arise and handle the new ground we are facing. This awakening can be rather uncomfortable because of our own internal struggles or the pushback we receive from others. Sometimes, it is much easier to simply run from the situation rather than figuring out why we are experiencing or feeling the discomfort or conflict. This shaking can also incite fear in our hearts, and it may even feel like our lives are in danger. But remember, God has shown us through His word and previous life experiences how to navigate danger and the unknown. God has equipped us with the tools, resources, and armor to take on battles each day.

Over the many seasons of our lives, the ground we stand on and the foundations we have built our lives on will shift.However, when we decide that above all things, we will build our lives on Jesus, the storms and changes of life will not destroy us.

Matthew 7:25 reminds us of this truth, *"The rain came down, the streams rose, and the winds blew and beat against that house; yet it did not fall, because it had its foundation on the rock."* When we stick with Jesus, we get a head start or, some would say, an unfair advantage that allows us to take our place as the ground shifts. In the midst of life's shaking and shifting, continue to look up, and you will soon find yourself walking on Hold ground.

PRAYER: Heavenly Father, I pray that You would shift the ground under me. Shift me out of the familiar and into the glorious destiny You designed for me so that I may take my position on Holy ground. Amen.

Reflection

ACTION STEP: What is stopping you from standing on Holy Ground?

Day 16
BECOMING MORE LIKE GOD

"Stop deceiving yourselves. If you think you are wise by this world's standards, you need to become a fool to be truly wise."
1 Corinthians 3:18 NLT

Passage of the Day: 1 Corinthians 3:18-21.

Miracles aren't designed to make us fit in with others or receive validation from the world around us. The opposite is true. When God blesses us with a miracle, we may begin to feel different from those around us because miracles often make us more like God. They usually draw us deeper into relationship with Him. Experiencing the power of God in our lives in a very personal way often makes us more curious about the things of God and things of the Spirit. As we begin to spend more time with God, we look more and more like Him. As a result of our new closeness with God, we also start to view the world around us differently. 1 Corinthians 3:18 states, *"Stop deceiving yourselves. If you think you are wise by this world's standards, you need to become a fool to be truly wise"*. What we once thought was important —like fitting in with others or being validated by others —no longer interests us. The wisdom of this world and the ways of this world become foolish to us.

As we continue to go deeper in our relationships with God, we must train ourselves to stop relying on those around us, the news, or social media to gain our knowledge during this time.

Remember, true knowledge, wisdom, and discernment comes from God.

PRAYER: God, continue to make me more like you and not like the world around me. Amen.

Reflection

ACTION STEP: In what ways do you see yourself becoming more like God?

Day 17
FAITH OR FEAR

"For God will never give you the spirit of fear, but the Holy Spirit who gives you mighty power, love, and self-control."
2 Timothy 1:7 TPT

Passage of the Day: 2 Timothy 1:7 and Hebrews 11:6.

re you in covenant with faith or fear?

According to the Merriam-Webster dictionary, a covenant is defined as: *"a formal and serious agreement or promise between two or more people, or a written agreement or promise usually under seal between two or more parties especially for the performance of some action."* Based on those definitions, I'll ask you our question of the day again —*are you in covenant with faith or fear?* Is the spirit of faith driving your decisions and directing your life? Or is the spirit of fear ruling your life? A covenant with faith allows us to live full lives under the lordship of the Holy Spirit. A covenant with faith also enables us to follow God's lead, speak up when God calls us to and empower us to create change in our personal lives and environments. On the contrary, a covenant with fear hinders us from doing what God calls us to do. The spirit of fear prevents us from following the voice of God —it forces us into silence when the Lord tells us to speak up and paralyzes us so that we don't have the courage to create change in our lives or communities.

When we operate from a spirit of fear instead of a spirit of faith, God often has to shake up our lives through crises or trials and tribulations to teach us that life is too short and far too precious to live in a constant state of fear. For example, some of us are reluctant to share our testimonies because we fear what people may say or think about us. However, to heal from our traumas and life experiences, we have to process and heal through them. One way we heal is by sharing our stories with others. Therefore, we are presented with two options —live in bondage to our life experiences out of fear, or speak out in faith and be freed through the sharing of our testimonies (see Revelations 12:11).

Next, let's consider the power of our words. The Bible teaches us that life or death lies in the power of our tongues. The tongue can be used as a tool of faith —when we speak faith, the earth listens, and deliverance springs forth into the hearts, minds, souls, and spirits of those in our environments. When we use our tongues as tools of faith —blessings are also spoken into the earth and secured through our words. When we live by faith, there is power in our words that makes hell nervous and silences the devil. But when the tongue is used to plant fear, the destruction we speak can spread quicker than a virus and can cause death to the minds, hearts, and spirits of everyone in earshot of our words. Are you speaking faith or fear?

If the recent COVID-19 global pandemic has taught us anything, it's that tomorrow is not promised —our lives can change right before our eyes in a blink of an eye. Life is too short to live in a constant state of fear or terror, worrying about what others think of us. The only person we should live to please is God. Hebrews 11:6 states, *"but without faith, it is impossible to please God."* We live lives that are pleasing to the Father by living our lives by faith. We can longer afford to be silenced by the spirit of fear.

We can no longer afford to remain stagnant or paralyzed by the spirit of fear. If the children of God do not rise and take their rightful places in society — if we continue to remain silent, things in the world will only get worse. We hold the answers that will heal our world. The Lord needs us to speak up and apply pressure. We are more equipped than we think we are.

I want to encourage us all to spend some time today talking with God, asking Him how we can apply pressure in this area of our lives? How can we live a life of faith? How can we fearlessly serve God's vision here on earth? What does He need us to do, or what does He want us to say to our friends, families, or in our communities? Our time to live fearless lives of faith is now!

PRAYER: God, help me speak up and speak out, and do what You want and need me to in the earth. Amen

Reflection

ACTION STEP: In which ways can you speak up in your life?

Day 18
MOVING IN THE DARK

"About midnight Paul and Silas were praying and singing hymns to God...."
Acts 16:25 NLT

Passage of the Day: Acts 16:16-40, Mark 15:33-47, and Mark 16.

When we retell the story of Christ's death, burial, and resurrection, we rarely acknowledge what happened in the middle. On a Friday afternoon, Jesus died on the cross and paid the debt for the sins of the world — past, present, and future. Then on Sunday morning, He rose again. But what happened in the middle? Was there a period of mourning and uncertainty for the disciples? Did Jesus' faithful followers struggle with their faith and disappointment because they just watched the Man they believed to be the promised Messiah die? The story of Jesus's death and glorious resurrection teaches us many lessons about the power of God and His faithfulness. However, this period between Friday and Sunday teaches us one very critical life lesson — God works in the dark.

Yes, God is the light of the world, but that truth doesn't mean we will not experience dark moments in life. God is always present with us, but it will not always be light in our lives when we see Him. The word of God teaches us that joy comes in the morning, but joy and salvation can also come in the midnight hour. We do not need to turn the lights on to see God. He can show us the way while leading us in the dark.

During the dark times in our lives, we must hold steadfast to our faith and trust that God is still moving and working in the background. Wherever we go in life —whatever we walk through —even the darkest of valleys — God goes before us, and His grace and mercy stand on guard behind us!

Right now, we are living through very dark times in the world. There may be times when we are praying but don't feel like we are receiving an answer from God. Even in those moments of silence, know that God is working. God's ways are not our ways, and His thoughts are not our thoughts. God works in mysterious ways, and He often uses darkness to lead us into the light. In the midst of darkness, when we can't see our way clear to God, we simply have to hold on to His written word and the promises He has already spoken over our lives. Sometimes we want confirmation from God that He is working, but the only confirmation we need is God is a man of His word.

Jesus rose on the third day just like He said he would. The journey getting there was a dark one, but, in the end, He won the victory over death, hell, and the grave! In Christ, we are promised that same victory. Whatever God said He would do in our lives, He will do. No matter how dark it is outside.

PRAYER: God, thank you for working in the dark! Amen.

Reflection

ACTION STEP: If you're experiencing trouble sleeping, use that time to talk to God. He wants to hear from you and spend time with you. Don't be afraid.

Day 19
PRAY WITHOUT CEASING

"Pray without ceasing."
1 Thessalonians 5:17 NLT

Passage of the Day: 1 Thessalonians 5:17.

Continuous seasons of unanswered prayers can cause us to experience faith fatigue or prayer fatigue. Faith fatigue happens when we've put all our trust in God and remained faithful to our belief in His ability to move in our lives, but the circumstances of our lives don't seem like they are changing. We experience prayer fatigue when we constantly pray to God, but it feels like He is not answering our prayers or talking back. Prayer fatigue can be identified by many symptoms as well. A prominent symptom of prayer fatigue is praying consistently or every day, but there's no actual faith behind those prayers. Then, we start struggling with finding the time to pray or the right words to say because God has been silent for so long, and honestly now, we may wonder what's the point? Prayer is a discipline, and it can be difficult to pray, especially when we feel as though God isn't answering our prayers. But I'm here to remind you that even though God is silent, He is working. He has heard your prayers, and His silence is golden. God's silence often means that He is working strategically behind the scenes. God has something amazing in store for us, and God's best takes time. At times, what God is preparing for us is so big, and as a result, it takes Him more time than we anticipated to iron out every detail of our blessings.

Big blessings take time. God's moments of silence may even represent a detour He has us on – a detour He is using to ultimately prepare us for what we've been praying for, plus more.

God is in the business of blessing us, but I also want to remind us that prayer is not about receiving blessings from God. Prayer is about spending time with God. When we love someone, we express our love in many ways, and one of those ways is by making time for them. Prayer is one of the ways we make time for God in our lives. Prayer is another way to show God His presence in our lives is important to us. Take some time to think about the last time your prayer was about serving God and God not serving yourself. Prayer should not always be about our wants and needs; it should also be about God's will. One of the most powerful prayers we can pray is, *"Lord, let Your will be done in my life."*

I believe God knew that we would experience many seasons of fatigue, weariness, and frustration on our spiritual walks. In preparation for these seasons, He left us scriptures like Galatians 6:9, *"And let us not grow weary of doing good, for in due season we will reap if we do not give up (ESV)."* He also ensured we had other scriptures of encouragement like Colossians 4:2, *"Be persistent and devoted to prayer, being alert and focused in your prayer life with an attitude of thanksgiving (AMP)."* Continue to wait and trust the Lord for His best, and hold on tight to His promises. Never stop praying, and when it is time, God will bless you.

PRAYER: God, increase my patience and faith. Amen.

Reflection

ACTION STEP: When was the last time your prayer was about serving God and not God serving yourself? When was the last time you prayed just to spend time with God, and how did you feel after that alone time with Him?

Day 20
DEATH

"And for your sakes, I'm glad I wasn't there, for now you will really believe. Come, let's go see him."
John 11:15 NLT

Passage of the Day: John 11 and Genesis 3:7.

In John Chapter 11, we read about Jesus' friend Lazarus, whom Jesus raised from the dead. Let me paint a picture for you. Jesus is traveling throughout the different regions of the ancient world, performing signs and miracles. Along His journey, He meets Lazarus and his two sisters, Mary and Martha. These siblings become very dear friends of Jesus. One day, Jesus received word from Mary and Martha that Lazarus was deathly ill and hurry back to their home to prevent his sickness from leading to death. Jesus gets this message and waits a few days before visiting Lazarus and his sisters. When Jesus finally decides to check on Lazarus, days have passed, and Lazarus has died, and he has been buried for four days.

When Jesus arrives in Lazarus' town, Lazarus' sisters are devastated because they knew if Jesus had just come sooner, Lazarus would have lived. However, Jesus reassures them that Lazarus will live again, and this testimony will be for the glory of God and to show all who are present that He is truly the Son of God. When they show Jesus Lazarus' resting place, He discovers a large stone covering the cave where Lazarus was laid to rest.

Jesus requests that the stone be removed but Martha objects, reminding Jesus that her brother has been dead for four days, and a terrible smell would overtake the people present if they were to remove the stone. Jesus replies again if they would only believe they would witness God's glory on the earth. The stone is rolled away from the cave, Jesus calls Lazarus forth, Lazarus walks out of the cave, and Jesus commands the people present to loose him and remove his grave clothes.

Mary and Martha wanted Jesus to hurry to their home to heal their brother from his illness, but God planned for an even bigger miracle to take place. Instead of healing their brother, Jesus wanted to show them the full power and glory of God. Yes, He could have healed their brother, but even better, He could raise him from the dead. Sometimes in life, God refuses to give us what we want because He plans to give us something better. The question we must ask ourselves is will we let Him?

Have you ever heard the term walking dead? The term is usually used to identify fictional zombies on television shows or movies, but I believe we encounter the walking dead every day of our lives —living people who are dead inside. We encounter men and women every day who appear to be full of life —Mr. or Mrs. Popularity or the life of the party. People who look like they are full of life but are actually dead inside. The deadness on the inside can be spiritual blindness, low self-esteem, depression, anxiety, hatred, jealousy, procrastination, lack of faith, and many more toxic traits or issues. Then, just like Lazarus, there can be a stone(s) covering us. The stone represents the clothes we wear, the number of likes or followers we have on Instagram, make-up, or anything else we use to cover up and hide the dead or broken places of our lives.

God is saying to us today, remove that stone and let Him help us. God has a blessing of healing and deliverance available to each one of us, but He is waiting for us to let Him into the dead and dark places of our lives. God is waiting for us to remove and let go of our stones so we experience true freedom and fullness of life. The stones we use to cover up are only temporary, but Jesus can permanently restore our lives and inner man far beyond what we have ever imagined.

We say we believe in God, and now it's time for us to believe in His glory and power and allow Him to help us. And whatever we want the Lord to do in our lives, we also have a part to play. If we want the Lord to resurrect the dead areas in our lives, we have to be willing to remove and give up our stones. Today, let's take some time to reflect on what is dead in our lives, the stones we have put in place to hide those dead areas, and the steps God wants us to take to remove the stones we have used to cover up.

PRAYER: Heavenly Father, shed light on what is dead in my life and show me how to take the necessary steps to remove the stone covering me. Amen.

Reflection

ACTION STEP: Take some time today to reflect. During your time of reflection, identify what is dead in your life and then take some steps to remove the stone before you.

Day 21
EXPRESSING
YOUR EMOTIONS

"Jesus wept."
John 11:35 NIV

Passage of the Day: John 11:18-35 and Hebrews 4:15-16.

Do you often find yourself suppressing your emotions because you're afraid of being labeled? You're afraid that those in your community or family will label you as weak, drama-filled, embarrassing, or even crazy because you are experiencing a moment of sadness, depression, or anger? Let's take it a step further. How often do we hold back our tears because we are ashamed of the pain or the hardships we face in life? Sometimes, we run from our feelings or emotions because we are embarrassed and struggle to take responsibility for the wrong, we've committed against ourselves or others. This embarrassment and shame can also keep us from taking responsibility for our sins and repenting for them.

Today, I want to encourage us to walk in our absolute truth and embrace our emotions. Our emotions are an internal indicator that signals when something is off in our lives. Instead of suppressing those emotions, we should sit with them, lean into them, process them, learn from them and then use them to take the necessary steps to make changes in our lives. It is okay to cry, and it is okay to feel remorse for our actions and repent.

If others want to label us based on the negative emotions we experience, that is okay too. Jesus was the Son of God, full of power, strength, and glory, but He still had the courage to weep. Jesus was no stranger to hurt, betrayal, and sorrow. He also knew how it felt to be forgotten by those He once helped and loved. Jesus was fully God and fully human — He understands the fullness of what it means to be human, and He cried too. If Jesus can cry, and feel a wide range of emotions, so can we.

Hebrews 4:15-16 states, *"For we do not have a high priest who is unable to empathize with our weaknesses, but we have one who has been tempted in every way, just as we are—yet he did not sin. Let us then approach God's throne of grace with confidence so that we may receive mercy and find grace to help us in our time of need."* Jesus understands our humanity, and He is always waiting to offer us support during our times of emotional distress and need. Sometimes, we suffer emotionally because we try to do things independently instead of asking God for help. Jesus wept before raising Lazarus from the dead. He cried and then displayed His power and majesty —imagine what He can do for us when we open up our hearts to Him. We cannot do this thing called life on our own. It's time for us to let go of our independence and let God be our support. It's time for us to start allowing God to walk with us intimately and talk with us. Sometimes our cries are more powerful than our prayers. The bible says God draws near to the brokenhearted (see Psalm 34:18), and the scriptures show us that Jesus has deep compassion for those He finds in seasons of pain or mourning (see Luke 7:11-17). It's time for us to open our hearts to God, share our emotions with Him, and invite Him into the intimate places of our lives. Don't be ashamed of the pain and hardships you face.

It is okay to share what is inside of you. Sometimes our greatest hardships produce our greatest and most effective testimonies, and God can use those testimonies to save someone's life.

Remember, what others think of you is none of your business, so who cares about a label. God for you is more than anyone against you!

PRAYER: God, I may not have the words to say, but I come to You with an open heart and welcome you into the intimate and painful areas of my life. In Jesus' name, Amen.

Reflection

ACTION STEP: Is there something you are trying to handle or carry on your own? If so, take the time today to ask Jesus for help.

Day 22
PAIN

"When the Lord saw her, his heart overflowed with compassion. "Don't cry!" he said. Then he walked over to the coffin and touched it, and the bearers stopped. "Young man," he said, "I tell you, get up."
Then the dead boy sat up and began to talk!
And Jesus gave him back to his mother."
Luke 7:13-15 NLT

Passage of the Day: Luke 7:11-17.

Sometimes in life, we experience different forms of pain that we never asked for (e.g., the death of a loved one, loss of a job, or a breakup, to name a few). These painful experiences can lead to stress, anxiety, depression, hopelessness, confusion, and a host of other negative emotions. Many of us have experienced one or all of those painful events or emotions during the COVID19 global pandemic. Those experiences combined with the length of the pandemic caused many of us to ask ourselves and God continually, when will all of this end? I wanted to remind us that sometimes life gives us unexpected pains, and in the same spirit of spontaneity, God can give us an unexpected blessing. God does more than just hear and record our prayers; He seeks to help us in our areas of need. We each hold a special place in God's heart, and every time we touch His heart with our cries and prayers, we should expect to feel His hand upon us, guiding us through this thing called life. When God sees our pain, He sets in motion a solution. When God has a feeling, action will surely follow.

In Luke 7:11-17, we get to witness Jesus show His compassion towards a widow by raising her only son from the dead without her having to ask. This passage of scripture shows us that we do not always have to ask to receive. That is the power of God's grace. Sometimes God uses tragedy to show us the power of His grace and to teach us to appreciate His grace. As Jesus leads us to the other side of our suffering, God's grace will carry us there.

PRAYER: Jesus, thank You for leading us to the other side with God's grace leading us there.

Reflection

ACTION STEP: What is currently causing you pain? How can you use this pain for something greater?

Day 23
EXPECTATIONS

"John's two disciples found Jesus and said to him,
"John the Baptist sent us to ask,
'Are you the Messiah we've been expecting,
or should we keep looking for someone else?'"
Luke 7:20 NLT

Passage of the Day: Luke 7:19-23.

Has there ever been a time in your life when you received something that didn't quite live up to your expectations? I'm sure we all have. For instance, we may hold a person in our lives to a high standard, but they fail to live up to our expectations. This has been a great struggle for me on my journey because I expect people to treat me the same way I treat them. Or I expect people to act a certain way, based on their position in my life. When those expectations are left unfulfilled, I start to question why God placed them in my life, and I often become quite doubtful of the relationship altogether. Or maybe you've consistently prayed protection prayers asking God to protect your family members and friends, but a loved one was recently diagnosed with the COVID19 virus or another illness. When we are met with failed expectations, we often begin to doubt God and His ability to move in our lives. These instances can leave us feeling lost, confused, and sometimes hopeless. If God is able, why does it seem like everything in life keeps taking a turn for the worse?

When we are met with these failed expectations or feelings of confusion or hopelessness, we should take our questions and complaints to God. For many of us, our initial instinct is to take our problems and concerns to our friends or family members, but I want to encourage us all to go to God first. In Luke chapter 7, that's precisely what John the Baptist did. John the Baptist was a faithful servant of God, and his faithfulness to God landed him in jail and ultimately led to his beheading and death. He sacrificed his life for what he believed in —the coming Savior of the world —Jesus. However, when faced with persecution and death, John started doubting everything he believed. So, he sent his disciplines to ask Jesus one question —*"Are you the Messiah we've been expecting, or should we keep looking for someone else?"* John wanted to know one thing —was Jesus the true Savior of the world. Instead of conversing with other spiritual leaders or his disciples, John took his questions and concerns directly to God. Ultimately, John wanted to know was his preaching, living, and all his sacrifices in vain. Jesus, the Son of God and true Savior of the world reassured John that He was the prophesied Messiah and John's death would not be in vain. When we have doubts or questions about what God is doing in the world around us or in our lives, we should follow the example of John the Baptist and take our doubts, questions, and concerns to God. He will provide us with the peace, clarity, or direction we desperately need and seek. And when life gives us hell, we mustn't forget that we are the sons and daughters of Heaven. God is a way-maker, and the sooner we take our problems to Him, the better. We shouldn't be afraid to have conversations with our Heavenly Father about how we genuinely feel. God wants an authentic and transparent relationship with us, so what's stopping us?

PRAYER: God, thank You for being a Way-maker. Thank You for seeking a continued relationship with me even when I tend to stray away. Amen.

Reflection

ACTION STEP: Do you take your problems to God or someone else?

Day 24
HELPING OTHERS

"Jesus knew what they were thinking, so he asked them,
"Why do you question this in your hearts?
Is it easier to say 'Your sins are forgiven,' or
'Stand up and walk'? "
Luke 5:22-23 NLT

Passage of the Day: Luke 5:17-26.

L uke 5:17-26 tells the story of Jesus healing a paralyzed man. News had spread that Jesus was in a nearby home healing the sick. The paralyzed man and the group of men helping him decided to travel to this home in hopes that Jesus could heal him. However, once they reached this home, they were met with a large crowd, and these men were unable to enter the house through the front entrance. In faith, the men decided to enter the home through the roof. Imagine these men removing tiles from the roof of a stranger's home and lowering their paralyzed friend down the roof and right in front of Jesus. These men were unable to provide their friend or family member with the adequate help he needed to be well, but they ensured he received the help he needed by any means necessary. Are you willing to go above and beyond to ensure your loved ones receive the help they need?

There may be people in your life that need some type of mental, physical, spiritual, emotional, or financial help or guidance. There are also individuals in our lives who are socially paralyzed because of the societal limits or labels that have been placed on them. These societal restraints can cause them to remain stagnant in many aspects of their lives.

Today, I want us to focus on the spiritual help that others may need. Many people have become hopeless and given up on God's promises. Some individuals struggle spiritually because they don't know how to go to Jesus for help. You may not believe it, but you can be the source of light and hope that someone needs in their life to keep going. You may wonder, how can I help those around me who are struggling spiritually. You can invite others to church, study through a Bible plan with your friends, share your testimony with someone, or pray for others. You never know how much these small acts of faith can help or even save a person. Recently, two of my best friends reminded me of the importance of continually praying for others. We are often unaware of what others are struggling with privately, and our private prayers for our loved ones can help save their lives in one way or another. We each face our own battles, trials, and tribulations in life, but I want to encourage us to ask God who we can help or pray for today.

I want to encourage us to take a moment and stop focusing on our struggles to help someone in their time of need. How can we help those who are unable to do what we can? Maybe it's not someone who is paralyzed in their body, but is there someone we can introduce to the Lord so that they can experience internal healing and renewal of a paralyzed spirit? Remember, someone else's faith blessed us at some point in our lives. Now it's our turn to be a blessing to someone in need. If our prayer life only consists of prayers about ourselves, that is a problem. God has called us to pray on behalf of others. Who can you pray for or bless today?

PRAYER: God, help me be a blessing onto others as You have so blessed me. Amen

Reflection

ACTION STEP: How can you be a blessing unto others? Is there currently someone who needs your help? Take some time today to say a prayer for them.

Day 25
THE HOLY SPIRIT

"The Spirit of the Lord is upon me, for he has anointed me to bring Good News to the poor.
He has sent me to proclaim that captives will be released, that the blind will see, that the oppressed will be set free."
Luke 4:18 NLT

Passage of the Day: Luke 4:14-21, John 14:16-17, and John 14:26.

J esus made it clear that the Holy Spirit is more than just an "it," a source of power, or a heavenly energy. The Holy Spirit is the third person of the Holy Trinity. God, Himself is three persons. He is one, yet three. He is our Heavenly Father, the One we love, fear, and obey. He is Jesus the Son, the One who we should emulate. And lastly, He is the Spirit, the One we should listen to and follow. John 14:16-17 states, *"And I will ask the Father, and He will give you another Advocate to help you and be with you forever— the Spirit of truth. The world cannot accept Him because it neither sees Him nor knows Him. But you know Him, for He lives with you and will be in you (NIV)."* The Holy Spirit is the Spirit that lives inside of us that gives us the ability to emulate Jesus Christ and live in a way that is pleasing to God. The Holy Spirit is our strength, He empowers us, and He helps us be and do. He allows us to walk fully in our identities as children of God, and He helps us fulfill our purposes here on earth. The Holy Spirit gives us the ability to enjoy the presence of Christ, and He teaches us all things related to God and things of the spirit.

He also gives us understanding when we misunderstand godly truths in the word of God. In addition, the blessing and gift of the Holy Spirit isn't just for us; it's for others as well. Through the Holy Spirit, we are given the desire to help others and the strength to even pray for our enemies.

Take a moment today to reflect on your relationship with the Holy Spirit and if you have been allowing the Holy Spirit to guide you the way God intended. Throughout your day, I pray that you would allow the Holy Spirit to fill you up in ways you never imagined. Don't be afraid to use the tools, armor, and resources God has equipped us with to make a change in our lives and a difference in the lives of those around us.

PRAYER: God, thank you for the Holy Spirit who is my strength. Amen.

Reflection

ACTION STEP: Reflect on your relationship with the Holy Spirit. Are you in tune with your third person?

Day 26

NO STRUGGLE, NO PROGRESS

"He taught regularly in their synagogues and was praised by everyone."
Luke 4:15 NLT

Passage of the Day: Luke 4:14-21.

If there is no struggle, there is no progress. Before we publicly worship, sometimes we have to struggle in private. Sometimes we have to catch some hell or walk through difficult seasons before we can minister to someone else or share our testimonies about what we have overcome. Jesus spent time in the wilderness before God sent Him out to complete His earthly ministry. He spent time in darkness before being the light of the world, and I believe we'll be required to do the same. Before God can use us to help others, He has to pull us away from the crowd to show us who we are and develop us into the people He desires for us to be. To receive the blessings we are seeking, we must first become people who can receive and steward those blessings well. Before telling others who to be or how to live for God, we must first deal with who we are. We cannot ask God to open doors for us if we refuse to close the doors in our lives that hinder our growth. Imagine being mad at someone else for living in their truth but refusing to address or deal with our own toxic traits that are hindering our growth or ability to walk in truth. Instead of admiring the word of God, we should try being the word. To see a change in society, we have to start with ourselves first.

PRAYER: Heavenly Father, help me become the person needed to receive Your blessings. Amen.

Reflection

ACTION STEP: What doors do you need to close that may be hindering your growth?

Day 27
HELP, PLEASE

"Then Jesus took her by the hand and said in a loud voice,
"My child, get up!"
Luke 8:54 NLT

Passage of the Day: Luke 8:41-56.

We can't do this thing called life on our own, but often, we can be stuck in our ways and too prideful to ask for help when we need it. We each wear many different hats and carry different levels of responsibility in our social circles. Sometimes, those perceived obligations or our self-sufficiency can deter us from asking God for help when we need it. In my personal life, this has been a great struggle for me. In my social circles, I am sometimes viewed and labeled as the *"strong friend."* The strong friend is usually the friend that appears to have it all together, rarely shows their emotions, and is the one who gives great advice to their friends and family. Everyone goes to the strong friend for help. This perception sometimes makes me feel like I have to be strong all the time because I don't want to be seen as weak by the friends or family members who rely on me. Instead of asking God or others for help, I usually try to bear the weight of my responsibilities on my own. However, I continue to find myself in a place where I realize I cannot do this thing called life on my own. I want to teach you what I've had to remind myself many times on my journey —when we need help, it is okay first to admit it and then ask for help.

I've learned to stop relying on myself and my logic and instead trust in and use my faith. Jesus wants to take over our lives completely, and we should let Him into our homes, hearts, and our lives. He wants to help us, and we should surrender control of our lives over to Him and allow Him to give us directions. It's okay to ask for help, strength, wisdom, discernment, clarity, and so on.

The funny thing is, we sometimes cry for Jesus to pick us up, and all we have to do is stand up and walk in the fullness of who He already created us to be through the Holy Spirit. We are already blessed with everything we need to receive the help we need in life, and all we have to do is yield to the Holy Spirit and allow Him to guide us the way God intended.

PRAYER: God, I cannot do this thing called life on my own. Allow Your will to be done in my life. Amen.

Reflection

ACTION STEP: What can you ask God for help with today?

Day 28
INDECISIVENESS

"Think about the things of heaven, not the things of earth."
Colossians 3:2 NLT

Passage of the Day: Colossians 3:2 and James 1:5-8.

L et's take a moment to think about indecisiveness and any struggles we have with making up our minds.
I often struggle with being indecisive, but I was reminded recently that we struggle with making up our minds due to the fear of making wrong decisions and the consequences that may occur because of them. For example, there are times when God instructs us to do something, but we might be afraid to do it because we begin to consider the friendships we might lose, or we fear that people will look at us differently. However, James 1:8 teaches us a double-minded person is unstable and restless in everything they think, feel or decide. We can't follow God and worry about how others will feel or think about us. We can only focus on pleasing God, or we will constantly find ourselves feeling unstable and restless. As we continue to grow in who we are and as God continues to establish us, we'll have to make hard decisions that we might not necessarily want to make. God wants us to be mature, stable, and established but do we want the same for ourselves?

As we reflect today, let's take the time to thank God for meeting us where we are.

Let's thank Him for His patience with all of our indecisiveness, depression, anxiety, and the stress we wrestle with when making decisions. After you thank Him, ask Him to elevate your mind to His level of understanding or perspective. Ask God to give you insight and show you His strategy for where you are right now and where He desires to take you. It's time we set our minds on the things above! Our minds are the foundation of who we are, and when God is preparing to transform our lives, He starts with our minds.

PRAYER: God, eliminate my indecisiveness and help me to trust that Your way is the best. Amen.

Reflection

ACTION STEP: What currently has you indecisive? Are you afraid of the consequences that may come with making these decisions?

Day 29
OPEN DOOR

"I know all the things you do, and I have opened a door for
you that no one can close.
You have little strength, yet you obeyed my word
and did not deny me."
Revelation 3:8 NLT

Passage of the Day: Revelation 3:7-13.

Jesus is opening up new doors of opportunity for His church, and it's time for us to walk through them. We live in a time of great possibilities, promises, and blessings. We were not created to be complacent, and we each have a mission to complete in our lives. As we step into what God has for us, some of us will have to fight against the naysayers and the people who constantly bring up our pasts or remind us of who we used to be. However, we cannot confine ourselves to how others define us or allow others to keep us bound to our past sins or mistakes. Jesus died for our sins and saved us from paying the debts for them. Whatever God has for you is for you, and your past mistakes cannot close the door to the future God has for you. Nobody can shut what God has already opened for you —including you. Whatever door(s) God is opening for you, walk through it with confidence, knowing that Jesus has His hands on you —guiding, protecting, and loving you. Be receptive to your open doors because God created you for more.

As you begin to walk through the doors of opportunities and blessings God designed for you, remember we also have a part to play on this journey. When we are blessed with more, we are obligated to do more. Obedience sets the stage for blessings. As we do what God tells us, the blessings will come. It's not always about what we accomplish; it's about what's in our hearts. Have we mastered faithfulness in our hearts? Have we learned faithfulness to God, His Word, and His process? When we are faithful, blessings will come.

PRAYER: Jesus, thank You for all the doors You opened in my life. Please continue to guide me every step of the way. Amen.

Reflection

ACTION STEP: What new opportunities or blessings are you welcoming into your life? How can you do your best to take advantage of these blessings while honoring God in the process?

Day 30
KEPT

"Because you have obeyed my command to persevere, I will protect you from the great time of testing that will come upon the whole world to test those who belong to this world."
Revelation 3:10 NLT

Passage of the Day: Revelation 3:7-13.

Each of us is currently running a race in life, and our race looks different from those around us. We all have different callings, needs and are equipped with various tools for success at different points in our lives. God equips us with the strength, patience, and courage we need to keep going throughout our races. We need God's power to press through the hard times. We also need God's strength because we cannot do this on our own. We may have the strength to make it through one day, but what about tomorrow —what about the rest of the journey? God also provides us with the patience we need to keep traveling on our race and the courage we need to keep going even when we do not hear from the Lord. While on our race, we also need to praise God, confess our faults or mistakes to Him and remain obedient to Him and His word. Those three steps are a part of the formula for success in our race. When we send praises up, God sends blessings and provisions down. When we confess our faults, mistakes, or thoughts to Him, God forgives us for our sins. And when we do what God says, He gives us what we need.

In this race or walk of faith, we may face trouble, hardships, trials, people hating on us, and more. However, throughout this race, one thing to remember is that we are kept by God. The race may be hard, but it will not overtake us. On your race, keep trusting, keep looking forward, don't stop, and don't worry. We are kept through God's grace, mercy, love, kindness, promises, and more.

PRAYER: God, thank you for keeping me! Amen

Reflection

ACTION STEP: Think of all the ways in which you are kept.

Day 31
CROWN

"Write this letter to the angel of the church in Philadelphia. This is the message from the one who is holy and true, the one who has the key of David. What he opens, no one can close; and what he closes, no one can open: "I know all the things you do, and I have opened a door for you that no one can close. You have little strength, yet you obeyed my word and did not deny me. Look, I will force those who belong to Satan's synagogue—those liars who say they are Jews but are not—to come and bow down at your feet. They will acknowledge that you are the ones I love. "Because you have obeyed my command to persevere, I will protect you from the great time of testing that will come upon the whole world to test those who belong to this world. I am coming soon. Hold on to what you have, so that no one will take away your crown."
Revelation 3:7-11 NLT

Passage of the Day: Revelation 3:7-11.

We were all fearfully and wonderfully made by God, and while He was designing each of us, He gave us unique gifts that He intended for us to use to make a difference in this world. Our gifts help us complete our earthly assignments and collaborate with God to complete His work here on Earth. Our gifts also allow us to be a blessing unto others. As we grow in our understanding of God and accept Jesus Christ as our Lord and Savior, God also places an invisible crown of righteousness on our heads. This crown represents the greatness on the inside of each of us and the anointing over our lives.

Each day as we go out into the world, this crown provides us with the power, favor, righteousness, and glory we need to move forward towards the completion of the tasks and purposes assigned to our lives. Biblically, this crown represents one of our rewards for our faithfulness and service to God, and we are all destined to have one of these crowns.

Today, I want to encourage you to hold on to your crown. Throughout our lives, the enemy will try to steal our crowns or trick us out of holding onto what God already said is ours, and he uses many schemes and tactics to do this. The enemy uses the allures and cares of this world in an attempt to have us forfeit our crowns. He tries to convince us to compromise our integrity, character, or relationships with God to obtain the things the world has to offer —money, power, notoriety, or success. But we are more than what the world or society says we are. Anything we receive from this world is only temporary. However, anything we receive from God — our heavenly rewards, lasts forever. The enemy also attacks our identity and purpose. He tries to block us from walking in the fullness of God by making us feel less than who God has called us to be, or he tries to make us feel like we are not qualified to complete the plans and purposes God has assigned to our lives. He also tries to make us think we have to earn this crown God promises to His children —he tries to blind us from seeing the truth about what God already said is ours.

The enemy is jealous of our position in the Kingdom of God, so he does anything in his power to make us lose our position by attacking our decision-making and behaviors in hopes that we will forfeit and lose what is rightfully ours. Although this crown is destined to be ours, we can still lose it. This is why we must remember what Jesus said, which is to hold onto our crowns, and we hold onto our crowns by holding on to Jesus. We hold on to Jesus by holding on to the promises of God —whatever God said in His Word; we can claim it now because it's already ours. If God says it's on the way, it's already here. If God says we can have it, we already possess it. Whatever we are struggling to possess, it is already ours. If we keep the faith, we do not have to compromise to possess what God says is ours —including our eternal crowns. We must hold on tightly to our crowns. Protect, cherish and appreciate your crown, and never take it off!

PRAYER: God, thank you for blessing me with my crown. Help me to hold on tightly to my crown and protect it. Amen

Reflection

ACTION STEP: Are you holding onto your crown? If not, what can you do to protect and hold on to it?

Day 32
TROUBLE

"Look! He comes with the clouds of heaven.
And everyone will see him— even those who pierced him.
And all the nations of the world will mourn for him. Yes!
Amen!"
Revelation 1:7 NLT

Passage of the Day: Revelation 1:1-8.

W hen we face trouble, trials, and tribulations in life, we are inclined to instantly avoid or try to escape the problems we are facing. We look for ways out of the ordeal or wish the trial never found us. Sometimes, we fail to realize that God is in the midst of trouble or a storm. Instead of trying to avoid or escape the trials or troubles we face in life, we should look for God in the midst of our circumstances. We should investigate the situation to see how God will move or use the situation for our good or development. Believe it or not, trials can help to bring out the best in us. Trials also help us develop powerful testimonies that we can share later to help others who are in need or in trouble.

Nothing that happens in our lives comes as a surprise to God; therefore, our trials, tribulations, and troubles do not move God. These moments are simply an opportunity for us to encounter God in a new and refreshing way. How will He meet us in the middle of this time of trouble, and how will He strategically guide us to the other side every step of the way? Some days may be more challenging than others, but remember to be patient, obedient, and remain focused on running your race. Whenever you feel discouraged, look up to the clouds (clouds represent the presence of the Lord) and smile. God is always with us, and He will never allow us to fall.

———————————

PRAYER: God, thank you for meeting me where I am, even when that means we are meeting in the midst of my troubles. Amen.

Reflection

ACTION STEP: Take some time today to enjoy nature. Focus on identifying how you sense God's presence in the world around you.

Day 33
SIN

"And I said to him, "Sir, you are the one who knows."
Then he said to me,
"These are the ones who died in the great tribulation.
They have washed their robes in the blood of the Lamb
and made them white."
Revelation 7:14 NLT

Passage of the Day: Revelation 7:9-17 and James 5:16.

I don't know about you, but sometimes I get uncomfortable talking about my sins because I don't want to be judged or looked at differently for my wrongdoings. However, if we ignore our sins instead of bringing them before God and others, sin can take control of our lives and lead us down paths of destruction. As we continue to sin, we also tend to isolate ourselves from God because we fear facing the consequences of our sins or simply having to talk with Him about what we did wrong. Now, I am not here to condemn you for your struggles or tell you to stop whatever you're doing that dishonors God or His word. And I am not saying that we have to be perfect. I think God knows we all fall short and will continue to fall short, and that's why Jesus Christ was the perfect sacrifice. He died for our past, present, *and* future sins.

Furthermore, everyone has a different walk of faith which includes their own trials, tribulations, and struggles with sin. The struggles we face today will form the testimony we'll use tomorrow to help someone else with their struggles and what they are going through. I am saying that we can't ignore our sins or run from God forever, and when we are ready to address our sins, God will be there for us and willing to help us overcome those sins. Remember, God wants to hear from us, and to grow in Him and who He wants us to be, we'll have to have some uncomfortable conversations from time to time.

God created us but lost us at one point because sin separates us from God. However, when Jesus died, that was God paying the ultimate price to buy us back —a life for a life —the life of His only Son for the lives of many sons and daughters. God is a God of grace, and even though He doesn't like sin, He still loves us! Run to Him, and He will give you freedom from your sins, and once He frees you, don't go back to situations you prayed yourself out of.

PRAYER: Heavenly Father, thank you for loving me even when I sin. I am far from perfect, but you still love me for who I am. Thank you. Amen.

Reflection

ACTION STEP: What uncomfortable conversation(s) do you need to have with God?

Day 34
THE SHADE OF GOD

"The Lord himself watches over you!
The Lord stands beside you as your protective shade."
Psalm 121:5 NLT

Passage of the Day: Psalm 121:5.

Psalm 121:5 states, *"The Lord Himself watches over you!*
The Lord stands beside you as your protective shade.
(NLT)" When I think of the shade of God, I think of God's protection. When we live and dwell in the shelter of the Most High, He promises to be our protection against the storms of life. His protection allows us to feel the warmth or heat of what is happening around us but ensures we never get burned or scorched in the fire. But what happens when we aren't under the shade of God? Simple answer — we get burned. And when we get burned, it sometimes causes us not to trust ourselves or God because we fear that God may treat us like the people or situations that burned us. However, I want to encourage us to remember that just because we have been burned, that does not mean we can't find future security or safety under the shade of God. Maybe God used the time we did get burned to teach or show us that we need Him. When we decide to live under the shade of God, we'll also discover that we don't have to experience the things that others go through, and even if we do, it doesn't impact us the same. In our experiences, we learn the difference between struggle and sacrifice. I believe that sacrifice is one of God's love languages. The struggles of life may teach us life lessons, but sacrifice builds us up and multiplies us.

When we live under the shade of God, we also learn to walk and talk differently. From this place of safety and intimacy, we start looking like true reflections and images of God. The Bible says we were made in the image of God, but throughout life, we have to live and act in a way that actually reflects His image. We learn who God is and how to be more like Him by spending time with Him. Today, take some time to sit with God and ask Him what you can sacrifice to reflect God's image better and continue to live in His shade.

PRAYER: God, thank you for Your continued protection as I live in Your shade. Amen.

Reflection

ACTION STEP: Today, take some time to sit with God and ask Him what you can sacrifice to reflect God's image better and continue to live in His shade.

Day 35
STRUGGLE

"You have patiently suffered for me without quitting."
Revelation 2:3 NLT

Passage of the Day: Revelation 2:1-7.

"*Without struggle, there is no progress*"—this is one of my favorite quotes to live by.

Life can sometimes feel like a constant struggle, as we face the many trials, hardships, and disappointments life often throws at us. When we decide to follow Christ, there are also troubles we have to face as children of God. Some of the battles we face in life are a result of the enemy we are fighting against—an enemy who is trying to steal our peace and joy. Or maybe we have to face off against the people who dislike us because we have changed our lives for the better. Or perhaps we are going through a storm because of someone we love and have committed to standing next to through the ups and downs of their life. During these times of trouble and hardship, remember that nothing worth having comes easy. Without that struggle, there will be no progression. At times, we even need the struggles of life to make it to the other side of our journeys —the other side representing the mountaintops of our lives or the abundance of blessings God has awaiting us. The struggles of life also grow our faith, mature our spirits, and teach us to appreciate that God is with us.

If you are currently going through something or maybe you know someone who is, I want to remind you of a few things: hold on to God and keep the faith; trouble doesn't last always; God has already defeated the enemy we are fighting against; struggle produces patience and obedience, and the blessings of life will always outweigh the struggles we face. In the midst of our trouble, we must also remember that God is not looking to see if we can win the war. He's looking to see if we are willing to show up for battle because He knows the battle is already won. We are already *more* than conquerors through Christ Jesus because of His love for us (Romans 8:37). We must never forget that!

PRAYER: God, thank you for every struggle I have faced in life because those struggles have produced within in me patience and increased my obedience towards You and Your word.

Reflection

ACTION STEP: What are you currently struggling with? What biblical truths or promises from God can you remind yourself of while facing these struggles?

Day 36
DRAMA-FREE

"Together they will go to war against the Lamb,
but the Lamb will defeat them because he is Lord of all Lords
and King of all kings.
And his called and chosen and faithful ones will be with him."
Revelation 17:14 NLT

Passage of the Day: Revelation 17:1-14.

Do you frequently choose peace over drama?

I've learned that we must place a high value on having true peace and joy in life. When we reach this point in our lives, where we value peace and joy above all things, we will quickly begin to see that everyone is not blessed with the same tools or values we now carry. We'll also notice that the way others act or behave does not align with who we have become. Some of those people will even choose to be mad at us for choosing to sustain our peace instead of engaging in drama or responding to them like we used to. There will come a time in each of our lives when we decide that it costs us too much to respond to people and situations the way we used to. And when I say *"it cost too much,"* I am not talking about money. I'm talking about evaluating what disturbs or compromises our peace and putting the necessary boundaries in place based on that evaluation. We must hold on tightly to our peace and joy by any means necessary and never allow anyone to take it from us.

We must remember that peace and joy are now our ultimate goals in life, and we'll need to exercise patience with others and obedience to our new lifestyle to sustain that peace.

Today, we live in a world where many people seek instant gratification and temporary satisfaction instead of doing the actual work to experience true and sustaining peace or joy in life. We encounter people daily who aren't honest about where they are in life, and lie and say they're happy just to make it by. However, their words and actions will reveal the truth about who they are and their internal struggles. When you are met with their negativity because of those unresolved internal struggles, remember to allow the light that shines down on you to also shine on them. There's no need to fight fire with fire. Instead, we can become more Christlike by being more loving, understanding, and compassionate towards others… while keeping our peace.

PRAYER: God, with trouble all around, thank You for the peace you continue to bless me with. Amen.

Reflection

ACTION STEP: Are you currently choosing peace over drama? Today, how can you be more Christlike (loving, understanding, and compassionate)?

Day 37
THUS SAID THE LORD

"When the people heard the sound of the rams' horns, they shouted as loud as they could. Suddenly, the walls of Jericho collapsed, and the Israelites charged straight into the town and captured it."
Joshua 6:20 NLT

Passage of the Day: Joshua 6:20.

Currently, where are you in your life? Are you walking in your purpose? Are you living a life of fulfillment, or do you feel stagnant? Do you feel like you're progressing, or are you constantly praying to God and feel as though He is not answering your prayers? For many of us, we may pray and ask God to bless our lives, but when it takes too long for those blessings to manifest, we may start to wonder if God is really listening or if those things will ever happen at all. We can rest assured that God hears all of our prayers, and every blessing happens according to His divine timing. Yes, God heard our prayers, but the real question we have to ask ourselves is, did we hear what He said? Did we hear the plans and directives He has given us to prepare us to receive those blessings we are praying for? And if we didn't hear God, is it because we aren't tuned into His voice, or is He communicating in a language we don't quickly understand? Today, I want to encourage you to pray for clarity and that Jesus would speak to you in a language you can understand and tune into.

The plans and purpose of God also run on circles and cycles, and He uses circles and cycles to birth new things into our lives. For example, there are cycles of unbelief and belief. Unbelief leads to wandering —wandering leads to distraction —distraction leads to desperation —and desperation leads to defeat. However, belief leads to obedience —obedience leads to faith —faith leads to confidence —and confidence leads to victory. On our journeys into the blessings of God, it's only a matter of time until we each experience a full circle moment in our lives. A full-circle moment represents that moment in our lives when the divine version of ourselves finishes what our belief started —a belief system that leads to victory in every area of our lives.

One of the greatest errors we can make is looking at our lives from the outside in. Before God can answer our prayers and change our lives, He usually changes who we are on the inside. What's happening on the outside will not change until we recognize the changes and development God is orchestrating on the inside of us. Have you acknowledged the inner changes you've experienced in your life? If so, know that your blessings are on the way. As we embark on a new day, let's get on the path to victory with our heads held up high. I pray you have a great day, filled with love, peace, joy, and the courage to ask God what He needs from you while also developing the patience and obedience to honor and fulfill His will for your life. I pray that His promises to you will fill you up and give you the push to keep going.

PRAYER: God, thank you for hearing my prayers. Help me yield more to Your voice and hear and understand You fully. Lord, strengthen my spiritual ear and speak to me in a language I can understand. In Jesus' name. Amen.

Reflection

ACTION STEP: What is God currently telling you to do to prepare for your future blessings?

Day 38
AUTHENTICITY

*"Then I began to weep bitterly
because no one was found worthy to open the scroll and read it."
Revelation 5:4 NLT*

Passage of the Day: Revelation 5:1-10.

It's so easy to lose sight of who we are because we so easily get caught up in who society tells us to be or lost underneath the many labels others place on us. Fear tells us to blend in when we were designed to stand out. And we join endless bandwagons, not realizing we were meant to overturn the wagon. We lose sight of purpose because the world convinces us to chase and follow our passions or titles. When we follow those societal trends and get lost in who the world tells us to be, we become deaf to the voice within that reminds us daily who we are, and eventually, we forget who we are.

Contrary to popular belief, the best thing we could do for our lives is embrace who God created us to be. To avoid losing our sense of identity, we should strive daily to be who God wants us to be and always live life from that place of identity. Instead of constantly trying to make ourselves over, we should embrace growing fully into who God created us to be. And sure, people may try to force us into a box of who they expect us to be. Or maybe they'll try to bring up our pasts in an attempt to remind us of who we used to be. When this happens, remind them that you are not your past, and they cannot hold you hostage to who you used to be. Remind them that you are striving daily to live as your authentic self, and you no longer feel the need to live up to anyone's expectations —including theirs. Then encourage them to also live from a place of authenticity. We should all be exactly who God called us to be. What others think of us is no longer any of our business. When it comes to being all God called us to be and receiving everything connected to that identity —we are no longer settling for the basement when our identification card gives us access to the penthouse!

PRAYER: God, please forgive me for every time I behaved or acted in a way that did not honor who You created me to be. Amen.

Reflection

ACTION STEP: In what ways do you feel like you are trying to live up to other people's expectations of you?

Day 39
TRYING FAITH

*"I know all the things you do, and I have opened
a door for you that no one can close.
You have little strength,
yet you obeyed my word and did not deny me."
Revelation 3:8 NLT*

Passage of the Day: Revelation 3:8.

Do you sometimes get upset with God because He didn't answer one of your prayers, or He is taking longer than expected to fulfill a promise He has spoken to you? I've experienced this frustration with God in my own life. Recently, I became upset with God because I was unable to accomplish something I believe He was leading me to do. I had to remind myself of His promises spoken to me at that moment. I also had to remind myself that when something doesn't go the way we planned, that means God has something bigger and greater in store for us.

Many things in life will test and try our faith, but waiting on the promises of God tests our faith consistently throughout our lives. When we are waiting on His promises, we should remember that the blessings God intended for us to receive, we will receive. God being for us will always be more than anything or anyone against us, and when God opens a door for us, no man can shut that door. When God says He has opened doors for us, that also means we can stop banging on closed doors. The promise may not come to pass when we want it to happen, but it will happen in God's timing.

If God says it will get done, we simply need to believe Him at His word. Ask God to replace those feelings with His promises whenever you feel your faith is being tried. Ask God to activate His Spirit within you and bring all your thoughts under submission to His Spirit. Ask God to control your thinking and intentionally set your mind on things above. Every day of our lives, we are standing on and in the promises of God. So stand firm and stand confident as you walk into the doors God is opening for you!

PRAYER: God, when I begin to fear that my life will never look like what You promised, please replace my fears with Your promises. Amen.

Reflection

ACTION STEP: Are you currently upset with God because He didn't do something you wanted Him to do or because He is taking longer than expected to fulfill His promises to you. Today, take some time to work through those feelings and share them with God.

Day 40
CLOSER TO CHRIST

"I, John, am your brother and your partner in suffering and in God's Kingdom and in the patient endurance to which Jesus calls us. I was exiled to the island of Patmos for preaching the word of God and for my testimony about Jesus."
Revelation 1:9 NLT

Passage of the Day: Revelation 1:9-18 and Matthew 16:24.

There is always more to learn about God than we currently know, and one way we learn more about God is by learning more about His son — Jesus Christ. God's presence also becomes evident in our lives when we intentionally do His will. There are times when we eagerly want Jesus to speak to us and tell us what He is doing in our lives. We don't want to hear the word of God from other people —we want to hear what will be done directly from Jesus. During these times, here are a few things to remember: to see Christ or hear from Him, we have to know Him intimately; to discover what He is going to do in our futures, we should investigate what He has already done in our pasts; and when we find ourselves in a bad place we should find ways to show gratitude because that opens up our world to new possibilities. Today, I challenge you to think about ways you can become closer to Christ and begin practicing and applying those ways into your daily life.

PRAYER: Jesus, thank you for all You have done in my life. Draw me closer to You. Amen.

Reflection

ACTION STEP: Today, I challenge you to think about ways you can become closer to Christ and begin practicing and applying those ways into your daily life.

Day 41
WHY SETTLE

"Immediately after this, Jesus insisted that his disciples get back into the boat and cross to the other side of the lake, while he sent the people home."
Matthew 14:22

Passage of the Day: Matthew 14:22-27.

H Have you ever experienced a time in your life when God instructed you to do something, and it led to some form of trouble or hardship? Do you ever feel like you're being obedient to God and His Word, but you are still experiencing challenge after challenge or trial after trial? During these moments, we may wonder —*"How much more of this can I take?" "Where is Jesus in all of this because this was His idea?" "Why is Jesus allowing me to go through this?" or "Does He really care about me?"* In Matthew Chapter 14, the disciples find themselves in the middle of a storm after obeying Jesus' command to get back into their boat and cross to the other side of a lake. In verse 27 of this chapter, Jesus encourages His disciples with these words, *"Don't be afraid. Take courage. I am here!"*

Jesus never promised that being one of His followers would be easy. He actually forewarns us by telling us that we will face many trials and sorrows on Earth. Then He encourages us by telling us to take heart because He has already overcome the world (see John 16:33). Being a follower of Christ isn't easy, but the benefits of this life are worth it. The blessings of a life in Christ far outweigh its hardships and difficulties. Some days, it may seem easier to simply live how we want to live, or it may seem easier to live a life that dishonors God and His word. But why settle for the temporary ease and satisfaction the world offers when God offers us a life that lasts beyond a lifetime? In the midst of your obedience and hardships, remember that God wouldn't lead us forward simply to watch us fail. He remains with us even in the midst of storms and troubles. We simply need to call on His name for help. As we continue to mature as believers and in our relationships with God, He also expects more from us, and He will stretch us by asking us to do more than we've ever done before. God's increased expectations of us will also require us to stand firm in our faith in Him and His word. As God begins to lead you into the deep waters of life, continue to walk by faith and not by sight, and remember Jesus is always walking with us.

———————————

PRAYER: God, help me to walk by faith and not by sight. Amen.

Reflection

ACTION STEP: Are you currently settling for temporary ease or satisfaction, or are you living a life that honors God and His Word?

Day 42
VOICES

"Anyone with ears to hear must listen to the Spirit and understand what he is saying to the churches. To everyone who is victorious I will give fruit from the tree of life in the paradise of God."
Revelation 2:7 NLT

Passage of the Day: Revelation 2:1-7 and John 10:4-5.

In our day to day lives, we are constantly fighting against the different voices competing for our attention. We are constantly wrestling against voices that make us feel anxious, voices that lead us back to old habits, and we even wrestle to hold on to the voice that brings us peace. Sometimes, we hear a voice that leads us forward, but then we find ourselves wrestling against confusion because there's another voice telling us to stay put. These voices can come from within, other people, the media, or even the songs we listen to. As one could imagine, hearing all these voices develops a problem in our lives because it becomes increasingly difficult to discern which voice is coming from God. We know that God is always speaking, but how do we locate His voice within the constant noise around us. The truth is —we don't have to beg God to speak to us. Sometimes, it's just easier to hear what other people are saying. Sometimes, we readily accept what others have to say because we simply like what they are saying better than we like what God is saying. Or maybe it's hard to hear and accept what God is promising to us. But we have to ask ourselves —is ignoring the voice of God and going for what feels better at the moment better than taking hold of the secret whispers and promises of God? Sure we may have to wait on the promises of God, but is that instant gratification better than what God has in store for us?

Today, ask Jesus to open your spiritual ears. Ask Him to bless you with ears to hear what He says to you. Ask Him to speak to you in a language you can understand and receive. As Jesus' voice slowly becomes the loudest voice in your life, be intentional about listening to what He has to say. Begin to listen and listen intently because walking and living by faith require us to hear what Jesus has to say. We can't grow in Christ if we refuse to tune into God's voice.

PRAYER: Heavenly Father, help me to discern between Your voice and the voices of others. Amen.

Reflection

ACTION STEP: Is instant gratification better than the promises God made to you?

Today, ask Jesus to open your spiritual ears. Ask Him to bless you with ears to hear what He says to you. Ask Him to speak to you in a language you can understand, to receive what He is saying to you.

Day 43
CHANGES

And the one sitting on the throne said,
"Look, I am making everything new!"
And then he said to me, "Write this down,
for what I tell you is trustworthy and true."
Revelation 21:5 NLT

Passage of the Day: Revelation 21:1-7.

We recently explored how we can draw closer to Christ and include intentional practices into our day to day lives that improve our intimacy with Christ. As a result, I've also been very intentional about developing my intimacy with Christ. I've been intentional about setting aside time each day to sit with God, be still in His presence, and overall I've been exploring creative ways to spend time with Him. These small changes have resulted in a huge impact. I have also been intentional about sharing with others the new things I am learning in my quiet time with God. For example, I've learned to focus on changing who I am inside, so those internal changes can impact and change what is happening around me. I've also learned to let go of the things that do not serve me. As we begin to let go of the things that do not serve us, we can focus more on what does serve us.

Life is all about change. When our lives are centered on God, we'll see that change is constantly happening in and around us. God is focused on getting us to where we are going, but He knows the changes we are making today prepare us for the blessings of our tomorrow. If we allow Him to, God will help us develop new ways of thinking, walking, and talking in preparation for our futures. Each day we should strive to be better than who we were yesterday. If we aren't intentional about making changes in our lives, we will struggle to experience positive growth in our lives. Today, take some time to sit with God and ask Him about some new changes you can start making in your life. Ask God what He needs you to work on in this season. Changes can feel scary, but would you rather grow with God or remain stagnant? The choice is always ours.

———————————

PRAYER: God, what do You need me to work on changing in this season? What are the changes you are calling me to make in my life? I am open to Your will and all new changes. Amen.

Reflection

ACTION STEP: Today, take some time to sit with God and ask Him to reveal some new changes you can start making in your life. Document or journal what changes you hear God communicating to you today. Then, ask God what He needs you to work on in this season.

Day 44
OVERCOMERS

"Look! I stand at the door and knock. If you hear my voice and open the door, I will come in, and we will share a meal together as friends."
Revelation 3:20 NLT

Passage of the Day: Revelation 3:20.

Do you consider yourself an overcomer? An overcomer is a person who endures and prevails against the spiritual, emotional, mental, and physical pain or trauma they have experienced in their lives. Take a moment to think about all you have overcome in your life. Now take a moment to identify how each of those situations was a blessing in disguise. Think about all the miracles that were birthed out of your painful experiences in the past. Think about the hidden opportunities that came from what you initially identified as an obstacle in your life. Now take a moment to thank God for using the good and the bad to bless your life.

In Matthew 16:24, Jesus states, *"Whoever wants to be my disciple must deny themselves and take up their cross and follow me (NIV)."* Galatians 2:20 states, *"I have been crucified with Christ, and I no longer live, but Christ lives in me (NIV). And 2 Timothy 2:11-12 states, "If we died with him, we will also live with him, if we endure, we will also reign with him...."* Based on these scriptures, as believers, we'll each have a cross we'll have to carry, a level of crucifixion we'll experience, and various forms of death and endurance we'll have to undergo during our time here on Earth. We have to go through what Christ went through to get to where He is. Our Lord struggled and overcame, and we shall do the same.

Being a follower of Christ comes with persecution, rejection, misunderstanding, and several different painful experiences, but in the end, it is all worth it. Everything we experience in life happens for a reason, and God has already conquered and overcome every trial or tribulation we could face in life. Think about the times you've encountered a battle and tried to fight it on your own. Then, God enters the fight and shows us how to win the battle and win the war. The struggles we face in life aren't easy, but we can find confidence in knowing that we are guaranteed to win every time as long as we live and fight God's way. And along the way, don't forget to take care of yourself spiritually, mentally, physically, and emotionally to be the best you each day.

PRAYER: God, thank You for all that I have overcome in my life. I give You thanks because I know my victories are only because of You! Amen.

Reflection

ACTION STEP: Today, how can you intentionally tend to your spiritual, mental, physical, and emotional health?

Day 45
JESUS SPEAKS

"Then a cloud overshadowed them,
and a voice from the cloud said,
"This is my dearly loved Son. Listen to him."
Mark 9:7 NLT

Passage of the Day: Mark 9:7 and Revelation 1:10-11.

C an you hear what Jesus is saying?

When we don't hear from God, we begin to wonder where He is — especially during times of trouble. When we feel like God is silent, it is critically important to be mindful of who we are listening to. Often people will attempt to tell us what God said, but everybody who talks about God is not actually hearing from Him. When we pray, it's also important that we wait to hear the Lord's response. Take a moment to assess your prayer time with God. Do you create the time and space to hear God's answer when you pray? Many of us don't.

Ask God to show you how to successfully talk to Him and then hear what He says to you throughout the day. God speaks to us in many different ways. Sometimes, He speaks to us directly, through other people, scriptures, music, posts, and so much more. Ask Jesus to speak to you in a way you can understand. Throughout your day, pray for a humble heart. Pray for spiritual vision and insight and the mind and eyes to see what is doing in your life.Ask God to show you signs of His presence in the world around you, and pray for wisdom and discernment to quickly identify those signs when He is talking to you. Then pray for the divine ability and strength to do what God calls you to do.

PRAYER: God, bless me with a humble heart. Bless me with the spiritual awareness I need to hear what You are saying. Lord bless me with spiritual vision and insight and the mind and eyes to see what you are doing in my life. Then give me the ability and strength to complete what You need me to do. I thank You in advance. In Jesus' name. Amen.

Reflection

ACTION STEP: Look for the multiple ways God has been speaking to you lately.

Day 46
UNSAFE SPACES

"I know that you live in the city where Satan has his throne, yet you have remained loyal to me. You refused to deny me even when Antipas, my faithful witness, was martyred among you there in Satan's city."
Revelation 2:13 NLT

Passage of the Day: Revelation 2:12-17.

Some believe that being a Christian means, we automatically escape the traps or hell the devil sets for us. Because we've been saved from sin and hell, we believe we'll never catch hell here on Earth as we graciously await our entry into Heaven for being the great people, we know we are. Now, that all sounds amazing, and in a perfect world, that could be so. But what happens when we take a step back into reality and find that God has allowed us to enter unsafe places? What if God wants us near Satan's throne and allows us to catch a little hell so that we can study our adversary and learn how to truly overcome and conquer him.

Running from the devil can sometimes cause us to miss our walk with the Lord. Before we enter any situation, God already knows what we are up against and wants us to stay to conquer and overcome the problem. Sometimes, He wants us to face our fears to teach us they aren't as terrifying as we initially thought. Sometimes, He wants us to stay so He can have a witness —a witness who will show lost souls that there is a will and a way out of every form of hell the enemy tries to plant us in. God is looking for people who will praise His name and stand their ground, even when they are in an unsafe place. God is with us and will give us the power to overcome any hell the devil throws at us. Then He will use our testimonies to be a blessing unto others. And if you need more proof, read Psalms 23:4-5 (KJV).

"Yea, though I walk through the valley of the shadow of death, I will fear no evil: for thou art with me; thy rod and thy staff they comfort me. Thou preparest a table before me in the presence of mine enemies: thou anointest my head with oil; my cup runneth over."

PRAYER: God, even in unsafe places, You keep me safe under Your grace and mercy. Thank You. Amen.

Reflection

ACTION STEP: Are you currently running from a place God is telling you to stay?

Day 47

RELIGION AND RIGHTEOUSNESS

"I know all the things you do, and I have opened a door for you that no one can close. You have little strength, yet you obeyed my word and did not deny me. Look, I will force those who belong to Satan's synagogue—those liars who say they are Jews but are not—to come and bow down at your feet.

They will acknowledge that you are the ones I love.

"Because you have obeyed my command to persevere, I will protect you from the great time of testing that will come upon the whole world to test those who belong to this world."

Revelation 3:8-10 NLT

Passage of the Day: Revelation 3:8-10.

C an religion get in the way of our righteousness?

There have been times when I've had conversations with people who do not attend church. When I would ask these individuals why they decided to stop attending church, I often heard stories about unresolved church hurt. Many of these people stopped attending church because of the people they encountered that made them feel less than welcome or less than worthy enough to have a relationship with God. I often felt confused because I was taught, we were supposed to enter into the Lord's House as we are. Over time, I realized that some people in the church can sometimes make others feel like they don't belong. Some of these people even think they know the Lord more than others or new believers because they've memorized a few or more than a few scriptures. Some people in the church also make others feel like the only way to walk with the Lord is to walk exactly like them. But everyone that attends church does not represent the true heart of God or Jesus Christ.

Matthew 7:21-23 states, *"Not everyone who says to me, 'Lord, Lord,' will enter the kingdom of Heaven, but the one who does the will of my Father who is in Heaven. On that day many will say to me, 'Lord, Lord, did we not prophesy in your name, and cast out demons in your name, and do many mighty works in your name?' And then will I declare to them, 'I never knew you; depart from me, you workers of lawlessness."* Just because someone talks about Heaven does not mean they are going. And sometimes, the same people who accuse others of running with the devil —are sometimes the ones being used by him.

Be wary of those who are stuck in religion. Remember in Matthew 17:20 when Jesus told His disciples they simply needed faith the size of a mustard seed to do mighty things. God cares about our faith. He does not measure how well we do church or perform in church, and He's not counting how many scriptures we know. Our knowledge of God is progressive, and with faithful intentionality, it grows over time. We do not need to be in first place. God cares about us staying in the race. Instead of looking down on each other in the church, we should focus our efforts on speaking words of encouragement. Speak the truth, but speak the truth in love. Love God and love others. Bless the name of the Lord, and speak blessings unto others. Be a blessing unto others, just as God uses others to bless you. Anybody, who tries their best to serve God and listen to the word of God, should be welcomed and loved by the community in the church.

If you have ever felt rejected by the church, I want to first apologize on behalf of the church as a whole. I also want to remind you that God loves you just as you are, and others can't dictate the personal relationship you have with Him. What someone says about you doesn't change how God feels about you. Your story may look different from others, but when you hold onto God's word, He will turn your story and flawed history into a testimony that will help other people!

PRAYER: God, thank you for allowing me to enter Your house the way I am. Amen.

Reflection

ACTION STEP: Is there anything currently stopping you from attending church? If not, how can you help others find a church home or help newcomers feel more welcomed in your church?

Day 48
HOPE

"We were given this hope when we were saved.
If we already have something, we don't need to hope for it.
But if we look forward to something we don't yet have, we
must wait patiently and confidently."
Romans 8:24-25 NLT

Passage of the Day: Romans 8:24-25.

Hope is defined as *a feeling of expectation and desire for a certain thing to happen.*
Hope is necessary in the life of every believer. When we find ourselves stuck in trying situations or circumstances we cannot escape, when our family and friends disappoint us, or even when God is silent — hope is what keeps us going. Think about the times you spent weeping throughout the night but held on to hope because you believed joy would come in the morning. Hope is the only thing that helps us when we're feeling helpless. Hope is how we made it in the past, how we maintain in the present, and how we will survive in the future.

However, I want to remind us to be careful not to misuse hope. In today's world, instant gratification has become a thing. Instead of waiting on what God has promised us, the idea of having it instantly overtakes us. As a result, we sometimes struggle with waiting on God, and some of us begin to manipulate the circumstances of our lives to receive desired outcomes.

Instead of waiting on God, we mistake the concept of hope with actively pursuing the things we desire and forcing them to happen outside of God's divine timing. Instead of rushing God's timing, we must wait and cooperate with Him. Sometimes, that also means actively waiting —doing something while we wait. Remember, faith without work is dead, and God actively prepares us for what we hope will come in the future.

PRAYER: God, increase my hope and strengthen my faith. Amen!

Reflection

ACTION STEP: The scriptures teach us that faith without work is dead —so what can you do now while you wait on God's promises?

Day 49
LOVE

"For God so loved the world, that he gave his only begotten Son, that whosoever believeth in him should not perish, but have everlasting life."
John 3:16 KJV

Passage of the Day: John 3:14-17 and Matthew 22:37-39.

Love can be difficult to find, but that does not stop us from relentlessly seeking to find love in the world around us. Some of us desire a certain type of love or a new love because the love we are currently experiencing doesn't feel right. Some hunger and thirst for love from others, failing to realize we already have the love we seek. John 3:16 serves as more than enough proof that God deeply loves every one of us and He loves us just the way we are. And the same God who first loved us desires for us to love Him too. The type of love we are seeking to receive from others, God first wants to receive from us. God is love, and our pursuit of love should begin with Him. When we focus on receiving God's love and then reciprocate that love towards Him, we begin to love ourselves and others the correct way. To love others properly, we must first love ourselves (see Matthew 22:39). However, our love for God should serve as the foundation of our love stories (see Matthew 22:37). If our love for God does not serve as the foundation for our romantic and platonic relationships, we will constantly find ourselves searching for love in the wrong places.

PRAYER: God, thank You for showing me how it feels to be loved. Show me how to imitate Your love and reciprocate it to You, myself, and others. Amen.

Reflection

ACTION STEP: Today, ask God to teach you how to love yourself and others the same way He loves you. In addition, how can you show yourself more love today?

Day 50
JOY

"Dear brothers and sisters, when troubles of any kind come your way, consider it an opportunity for great joy. For you know that when your faith is tested, your endurance has a chance to grow. So let it grow, for when your endurance is fully developed, you will be perfect and complete, needing nothing."
James 1:2-4 NLT

Passage of the Day: James 1:1-4 and Psalms 96:9-13.

We often look for joy in all the wrong places. Some people believe we only experience joy when we have a lot of money, drive a nice car, wear designer clothes, and so on. It's a blessing to have these things, but what happens when our joy is rooted in having those blessings versus the God who gave them to us? When we live this way, we tend to miss out on the unshakable joy of the Lord that is promised to all believers. When we take our focus off of God, our joy can be easily shaken by the circumstances of our lives and the world events happening around us. For example, when we think about the joy of Christmas. Many of us get wrapped up in the excitement of receiving a ton of gifts or decorating our homes and Christmas trees. Consequently, we forget all about the *Christ* in Christ-mas.

Despite what we may possess in life (i.e., money, cars, designer clothes) and what may be going on in our lives, we must take the time to find joy in the small things and acknowledge what God is doing in our lives. Even if we find ourselves tested by financial troubles, family drama, or heartbreak, count that as joy. Remember, joy comes in the morning, and I believe God gives us an opportunity to start each day with our cups full of joy.

PRAYER: God, thank you for the joy that comes in the morning! Amen.

Reflection

ACTION STEP: Despite what you may be going through in your life, take the time to find joy in the small things and acknowledge and give thanks for what God is doing in your life.

Day 51
PEACE

"I am leaving you with a gift—peace of mind and heart.
And the peace I give is a gift the world cannot give.
So don't be troubled or afraid."
John 14:27 NLT

Passage of the Day: Isaiah 9:6-7 and Matthew 2:1-18.

We know God is the Prince of Peace but is He also the Disturber of Peace? I believe He is. God often uses the storms and trials of life to mature and develop His children (see James 1:2-4). A disturbance in our peace can often mean that change is on the horizon. Sometimes God uses storms to prepare us for the blessings that are to come. He'll shake up the world around us to tear down what shouldn't be and then build up what should. In addition, I believe God places us in storms on behalf of others because they are not strong enough to fight or handle the storm themselves. However, He also blesses us with peace in the midst of every storm we face in life.

God sees us as strong through Christ Jesus, and He knows we can endure and withstand any test or trial thrown our way. Furthermore, our tests and trials produce the testimonies we share with others. Testimonies that attest to the wonderful works of our Lord. When your peace is disturbed, take a moment to investigate if God is standing in the fire with you. Don't automatically rebuke your storm, view it as a negative, or label it a test from the devil (We give the devil too much credit for disturbing our peace and causing chaos in our lives). Look for God in the middle of your circumstances and see the disturbance as evidence that God is about to take you to the next level. No matter the storm, God will bless us with peace in the midst of it.

So how's your peace?

PRAYER: God, thank You for all the storms I have been in. Whether they were for me or someone else, I thank You! Amen

Reflection

ACTION STEP: How have the storms you've faced in life matured you or developed you?

Day 52
TAKING A STEP BACK

*"That day the Spirit led him to the Temple.
So when Mary and Joseph came to present the baby Jesus to
the Lord as the law required, Simeon was there. He took the
child in his arms and praised God, saying,
"Sovereign Lord, now let your servant die in peace, as you
have promised. I have seen your salvation,"
Luke 2:27-30 NLT*

Passage of the Day: Luke 2:21-32.

When was the last time you took a step back to address your spiritual, mental, physical, and emotional health? When was the last time you took a step back to spend time with God? Have you taken the time to hear what God needs and wants from you? Have you developed a habit of waiting on God before you act, or do you more often than not decide independently and take matters into your own hands? Whatever your answers to these questions may be, I want to remind you that there is more to life than your experiences or intellectual knowledge, and God has a predestined plan assigned to your life. Make it a life practice to frequently check in with God and ask Him why He created you and what you are supposed to do with your life. Due to the COVID19 global pandemic, the last few years haven't been ideal for most people. However, our duty as Kingdom ambassadors is to discover what God is still trying to show us. God did not bring us this far for no reason. We have a purpose assigned to our lives, and it's up to us to choose if we will use our time here on Earth wisely!

PRAYER: Heavenly Father, help me finish the work you have assigned for me to complete here on Earth. Show me the work You need me to address this year. Show me how to eliminate all laziness and procrastination from my life. In exchange, bless me with the motivation and strength I need to pursue my purpose. In Jesus' name. Amen.

Reflection

ACTION STEP: When was the last time you took a step back to address your spiritual, mental, physical, and emotional health?

When was the last time you took a step back to spend time with God?

Have you taken the time to hear what God needs and wants from you?

Have you developed a habit of waiting on God before you act, or do you more often than not decide independently and take matters into your own hands?

Day 53
SALT AND LIGHT

"You are the salt of the Earth. But what good is salt if it has lost its flavor?
Can you make it salty again? It will be thrown out and trampled underfoot as worthless.
"You are the light of the world—like a city on a hilltop that cannot be hidden.
No one lights a lamp and then puts it under a basket.
Instead, a lamp is placed on a stand, where it gives light to everyone in the house.
In the same way, let your good deeds shine out for all to see so that everyone will praise your heavenly Father."
Matthew 5:13-16 NLT

Passage of the Day: Matthew 5:13-16.

What good is salt if it has lost its flavor or light that cannot be seen? As believers and Kingdom ambassadors here on Earth, it's important that we consistently check ourselves to ensure we are showing up in the world as God intended. Here are a few questions we can ask ourselves:

• Are we focused on being the salt of the Earth and adding the needed flavor and seasoning to our relationships and environments? Or are we too busy trying to fit in or be a socialite?

• Have we made a habit of spreading light everywhere we go, or are we more concerned with being in the spotlight or the center of attention?

• Are we focused on making our names great or Jesus' name great?

• Have we become accustomed to looking for handouts rather than utilizing what God has placed in our hands?

Remember, God, placed us here on Earth for a reason. We all have a purpose, and it's time to make use of it. We are called to make a difference in the world. When others see us, they should see God. Our devotion to God should impact how we walk, talk, think, and act. When we enter or exit a room, people should feel the effects of our presence and absence. The time is now for us to get into our bag, walk in our purpose and align with God's will. It is important to live our lives to the fullest, but are we really living life to the fullest if we live it outside God's will?

———————————

PRAYER: God, help me to be the salt of the Earth and light of the world. Amen

Reflection

ACTION STEP: How can you begin to make a difference in the world?

Day 54
COOPERATING WITH GOD

"So for the second time they called in the man who had been blind and told him,
"God should get the glory for this, because we know this man Jesus is a sinner."
"I don't know whether he is a sinner," the man replied.
"But I know this: I was blind, and now I can see!"
John 9:24-25 NLT

Passage of the Day: John 9:1-7 and Luke 9: 24-25.

What's happening in our lives when we pray for miracles but they do not happen? We pray and talk to God, read our bibles, tithe, help or serve others, and we try our best to live in a way that honors God —yet our miracles do not happen. A possible answer —we are not cooperating with God. Maybe we don't see miracles in our lives because God is waiting for us to move. God will not do for us what we can do for ourselves. For instance, He can help us get the job or degree, but He can't study for us, research the job logistics, or update our resumes. If we want to see miracles manifest in our lives, we have to play our part and do the things God is asking us to do. It is also encouraging to know that He provides us with the guidance we need to complete those tasks. However, many people choose ignorance over elevation. Instead of discovering and acknowledging what God is asking them to do, they choose to remain blind because we sometimes find bliss in ignorance. Our safe zones often bring us joy and comfort, but staying in the safe zone also means we remain stagnant. If we want more, God will require more from us.

Living a full life —a life of purpose and abundance requires some work. God wants us to live our best lives, but that life requires us to walk in purpose and follow His will. If we're going to experience life-altering changes in our lives, it starts with recognizing we need to change and then cooperating with God to facilitate it.

———————————————

PRAYER: Heavenly Father, help me step out of my comfort zone. Teach me how to welcome and accept change, and show me how I need to cooperate with You to carry out Your will for my life. Amen.

Reflection

ACTION STEP: In what ways can you cooperate better with God?

Day 55
SHOW AND PROVE

"She tormented him with her nagging day after day until he was sick to death of it."
Judges 16:16 NLT

Passage of the Day: Judges 16:16.

When God makes a promise to us, we often begin to wonder —when, where, and how this promise will come to pass. In addition, we may start to wonder if there is anything we need to do for this promise to manifest in our lives. Does God want us to move forward in pursuit of the promise, or does He want us to be still and wait on Him?

Throughout my life, I have learned that the changes we are implementing in our lives now —prepare us for the blessings awaiting us in our futures. As God begins to build and prepare us for His promises, we should start moving differently as individuals. We should be more careful about the choices we make, the people we hang with, and we should begin to leave old habits behind. In these moments, we should be seeking God first and doing what He needs us to do to prepare our lives for the promise. These changes and refined choices build a bridge in our lives that gets us closer and closer to the promise. But what happens when we find ourselves stuck in the middle of who we used to be and who God is calling us to be? What happens when the wait becomes challenging, and we begin to go rogue and live in a way that communicates to God that we no longer need His help?

The middle can lead us into a state where we feel isolated, uncomfortable, and lost. We may not hear God's voice as much as we used to, and it could be because our voice has taken over. We have to stop and honestly identify where we are during these moments. Then, we should ask God to show us what He is doing and if He is moving in a new direction. Are we trying to build another bridge to make it to this promise when God is extending new grace as He offers a tightrope? The tightrope in this scenario represents the shift or pivot God has made on the way to the promise. The tightrope also represents a place in our lives where we have to trust God a little more because He is stretching our trust and faith in Him. When we notice that God has made this pivot, we should take our focus off of the promise and focus our efforts on discerning what God is trying to show us in our lives at this moment. It's okay to remember God's promises, but we also have to focus on what He is trying to do in our lives now and what He wants us to work on internally and externally. God wouldn't allow us to walk on that tightrope to fall. When the Lord says go, He goes with us. The Lord stands by us, gives us power, strength, and peace in the stretching.

PRAYER: Heavenly Father, thank you for walking with me on this tightrope. Your safety net of grace and security is ever-present during my times of stretching. Even when I may slip or tumble, You pick me right back up. Please help me to keep going. Amen.

Reflection

ACTION STEP: Focus on the now and not the next. What is God showing you right now?

Day 56
THE RIGHT WAY

"But when you pray, go away by yourself, shut the door behind you, and pray to your Father in private. Then your Father, who sees everything, will reward you."
Matthew 6:6 NLT

Passage of the Day: Matthew 6:5-13.

Have you ever wondered if you're praying the right way? If you have ever had a *"does God hear my prayers"* moment, it may be time to try a new prayer strategy and ask the Lord to teach you how to pray. Similar to the original disciples, we can also ask Jesus to show us how to pray. We can also ask the Lord what words to say when we pray and the method of prayer we should use to get Heaven's attention. Don't be afraid to ask Jesus how we should pray to ensure God hears and answers us.

Prayer is not just about talking; it's about Who we are talking to. Prayer should become a daily habit in the life of all believers and not simply something we do when we are in trouble or when it is convenient for us. Prayer is an excellent time to talk to God about ourselves, the desires of our heart, and a time to lift others up in prayer. While praying, we should not worry about our troubles or the cares of this world and trust that God already has those areas of our lives taken care of. We should focus our prayers on things only God can do for us —things that are eternal and will help us bear fruit. The benefits of praying are endless as well — prayer makes us stronger, makes room for divine peace in our lives, gets

Heaven's attention, and helps us to discern God's will for our lives. Remember, prayer is powerful because we are talking to a powerful God. Prayer can move God, and God can move anything.

PRAYER: Lord, teach me how to pray effective prayers. Amen.

Reflection

ACTION STEP: Read Luke 11:1-10.

Day 57
BENEFITS OF SERVING

"Jesus told the servants, "Fill the jars with water."
When the jars had been filled, he said, "Now dip some out,
and take it to the master of ceremonies." So the servants
followed his instructions."
John 2:7-8 NLT

Passage of the Day: John 2:1-10.

A servant can be defined as a person who performs duties for others or a devoted and helpful follower or supporter of another. There are many benefits we gain from serving others. For example, sometimes God uses positions of servitude to train and equip us for positions we will hold later in life. We also learn more about the heart of God and how to sacrificially love people when we serve. However, serving is not easy. As we serve, God sometimes instructs us to do things we simply do not want to do or agree with. Instead of obeying His commandments, we may choose to discuss or debate with God about what He is asking us to do. We use this dialogue to talk or bargain our way out of a command or task. We may find it difficult to obey God because of our logic, and we may even discuss the matter with others in hopes that they will agree with us or help us make sense of what God is telling us to do. But we do not need to do any of this. All we need to do is follow orders and be obedient. We will never learn the secrets of God if we constantly feel the need to discuss logic and logistics with God.

To serve successfully, we must humble ourselves before God. We do this by submitting our will and control over our lives to God. Living from this place of submission then allows God's will to be done in our lives without resistance or hindrance.

PRAYER: God, how can I better serve you today? Show me how to be a blessing unto others successfully, and complete the assignments you have set before me. Amen.

Reflection

ACTION STEP: Take a moment to reflect and ask yourself if you're truly serving God and being obedient to what He is instructing you to do. Once you identify where you are and find out what God is leading you to do in this season — just do it. Don't ask why.

P.S. If your obedience to God leads you into a season of isolation and separation from others, don't worry because this can result from serving as well.

Day 58
THE DOOR

"I am the door: by me if any man enters in, he shall be saved,
and shall go in and out, and find pasture."
John 10:9 KJV

Passage of the Day: John 10:1-9.

On this walk of life, we may choose to enter through many doors in hopes that they will take us to the next level in our lives. We sometimes take matters into our own hands, create our own wills for our lives, and then hope that God will support us in our choice to open and walk through doors without Him. But if we want to experience all this life has to offer us and all that God desires to give us, we must remember that Jesus is the door we should constantly find ourselves in front of. Jesus is our way in and our way out. To make contact with God and gain access to the blessings of God, we must go through Jesus. He is the only way we can truly know God as a Father. Jesus is the way, the truth, and the life. Once we enter through His door, we must also understand that this choice will forever change our lives from that moment on. We can focus on things eternal and not temporary, and we will not lack or need anything. All the weapons forming against us and prospering will no longer do so because we are now behind Christ's door of protection. The peace and joy we've been searching for in life are also behind this door. We may have opened many doors in our lives, but nothing compares to the door named Jesus Christ.

PRAYER: Jesus, thank you for being the Way, the Truth, and the Life! Amen.

Reflection

ACTION STEP: Are there any doors you are currently opening without God?

Day 59
ARE YOU FOR OR AGAINST JESUS?

"Anyone who isn't with me opposes me,
and anyone who isn't working with me is actually working
against me."
Luke 11:23 NLT

Passage of the Day: Luke 11:14-23 and Revelations 3:20

Yesterday, we spoke about Jesus being The Door into the life God planned for us.
But, what happens when He knocks on the door of our hearts? Do we answer or ignore it? We have the free will to choose whether or not to let Jesus into the doors of our lives, but we cannot be neutral in this decision. In addition, we cannot open the door halfway and expect all of God's blessings to flow in. If we choose to open this door, we must open it all the way. Sometimes, we struggle to let Jesus into our lives because we do not want to give up certain things in our lives. Especially if we have become accustomed to a particular lifestyle. However, I want to remind us that when we choose Jesus, a relationship with Him comes with everything we need. We can't let the attractions of this world cause us to lose sight of what is important in life. Our old lifestyles and what the world offers are temporary, whereas God promises us blessings in this life and the one hereafter. The blessings of God are also eternal.

It's never too late to answer when Jesus comes knocking, but when you answer, get ready to live a life that is fully committed to Him.

PRAYER: Jesus, thank You for knocking on the door of my life. Help me to always answer when You come knocking. Amen.

Reflection

ACTION STEP: When Jesus comes knocking on the door of your heart/life, will you answer His knock or ignore Him? Is there anything that would help you to answer Him readily?

Day 60
TRUST GOD

"But we have only five loaves of bread and two fish!"
they answered."
Matthew 14:17 NLT

Passage of the Day: John 6:1-15 and Matthew 14:13-18.

When we face problems or issues in life, it's important that we clearly identify the issue, take it to God in, prayer and then wait in hopeful expectation for the blessing or solution to appear. Along with identifying the problem and bringing it to God in prayer, we must also prepare for the possibility that God may ask us to serve and act as part of the solution. For example, for those of us who desire to create legacies of generational wealth in our families to solve the issue of chronic poverty or lack —God may ask us to start a business. For those praying for reconciliation for broken families —God may ask us to start the healing journey within ourselves before He sends us back to our families. When we ask God for a blessing or to solve a problem in our lives, we have to be open and willing to sacrifice to be a part of the solution. We've come to God and given Him all the facts about the matter, but do we have faith in God and trust Him enough to do what He may ask us to do? God often places all the pieces of the puzzle right in front of us, so why do we constantly find ourselves before Him asking for more? Do we not trust that the pieces God has given us are enough?

To experience a breakthrough in our lives, we must trust that God knows what He is doing. Think about all that you've overcome or accomplished in your life. If God ordained our steps and allowed us to make it this far in life, why would He fail us now? When we learn to trust God with what we have and who He has called us to be —we will find out that we actually have more than we thought or imagined.

PRAYER: God, thank You for the little that I have. I trust and know You can turn it into something bigger and grander! Amen

Reflection

ACTION STEP: Do you trust God with what you have?

Day 61
KEEP GOING

"Write this letter to the angel of the church in Smyrna. This is the message from the one who is the First and the Last, who was dead but is now alive: "I know about your suffering and your poverty—but you are rich! I know the blasphemy of those opposing you. They say they are Jews, but they are not, because their synagogue belongs to Satan. Don't be afraid of what you are about to suffer. The devil will throw some of you into prison to test you. You will suffer for ten days. But if you remain faithful even when facing death, I will give you the crown of life. "Anyone with ears to hear must listen to the Spirit and understand what he is saying to the churches. Whoever is victorious will not be harmed by the second death."
Revelation 2:8-11 NLT

Passage of the Day: Revelation 2:8-11.

It's not easy being a follower of Christ. We experience many tests and storms that seek to turn our lives upside down on this journey. We may feel like giving up on God and ourselves during these times because we can no longer see the finish line to our race. When you feel like you no longer have the strength to go forward, remember the faithfulness of God. He is always right there with us in the midst of our storms . Rather than running back to old habits to escape our problems, we have to learn to endure the pressures of life.

If we can't handle the pressures of life, how can God use or bless us? The word *"trouble"* frequently carries a negative connotation. However, when God is involved, He uses what the world views as unfavorable for our good. Instead of fearing trouble or hardships, we should see it as a challenge and opportunity to grow in God and ourselves. God is playing chess, and He knows how to use that trouble to bless us.

One last thing — some of the tests or trials we endure may not be for us. God may require us to go through certain test or trials on behalf of our loved ones because they aren't strong enough to handle it —but we are. God gives His toughest battles to His strongest soldiers, and we are each much stronger than we think we are!

PRAYER: God, even though I cannot see the finish line, help me to keep going! Amen.

Reflection

ACTION STEP: What motivates you to keep going when you feel like giving up?

Day 62
LIFE AND DEATH

*"I tell you the truth, unless a kernel of wheat is planted in the
soil and dies, it remains alone.
But its death will produce many new kernels—a plentiful
harvest of new lives."
John 12:24 NLT*

Passage of the Day: John 12:20-26.

U sually, when we think of seasons changing, we may think about the weather, changing out our spring and summer wardrobes for our fall and winter ones, and more or fewer outside activities. Seasons are also known for what dies off or comes to life in a given season. In our lives, whether literally or figuratively, we experience these same cycles of life and death. And there is such a negative connotation associated with death, but what if death meant fulfillment?

Have you ever wondered what's your purpose or calling in life? Have there been times you felt stuck or almost like you were drowning? You continued asking God for help, but it felt like those prayers weren't being answered, and you began to sink further into confusion and despair? We are taught to seek God in our times of need, but what happens when God is waiting for us so He can move? God hears our prayers and wants to give us all we need and desire, but what happens when we haven't made room for Him to move in our lives? As human beings, we are often resistant to change, and sometimes we are committed and loyal to our old habits, even when they no longer serve us.

More often than not, we refuse to let the old versions of ourselves die and consequently miss out on who God called us to be in life. How do we expect to move forward into the future if we are stuck in the past? God is waiting to give us the power and authority we need to move forward in our lives, callings, and futures. However, He needs us to cooperate with Him. When we allow the old version of ourselves to die, we ultimately make room for God to transform us and deposit into us what we need for the new season in our lives.

Today, take some time to sit with God and talk to Him. Ask God to show you what He needs you to do to walk into the next season of your life. Maybe you need to fast from certain things, spend more time with Him in prayer, read weekly Bible plans, worship more, or separate yourself from certain people. Whatever God asks you to do, know that you are one step closer to creating room for God to help you grow and move you into your destiny!

PRAYER: God, show me how to make room for You in my life and create a lifestyle that will help me grow into the person You need and want me to be. Amen.

Reflection

ACTION STEP: Today, take time to sit and reflect on what holds you back in life. Ask God to show you what He needs you to do and change in your life to prepare for your next season.

Day 63
BE YOURSELF

"The rain and snow come down from the heavens and stay on the ground to water the earth. They cause the grain to grow, producing seed for the farmer and bread for the hungry."
Isaiah 55:10 NLT

Passage of the Day: Isaiah 55:10-11.

It can be quite easy to lose focus of who we are in today's society. There are also many factors in life that can cause us to hide who we are. Maybe we are experiencing what feels like stagnation in our lives while simultaneously watching everyone else around us succeed. This feeling of stagnation mixed with thoughts of comparison can also tempt us into taking shortcuts to get where we are trying to go — faster. We may even settle for moments or experiences that lead to instant gratification to appear successful in our hearts and in the eyes of others. However, when we operate outside of the Lord's will and begin to receive praise from others for being someone God did not call us to be, we can quickly lose sight of who we are. But I am thankful that even when we forget who we are, God still knows who we are, and He is always waiting to remind us. We are the same people God spoke a word into before He placed us in our mothers' wombs. When God spoke a word into us, He left it empty, so through our lives, we could bring it back to Him complete. To do this, we have to be our authentic selves —the person God created us to be.

It's time to remove the mold or shelf of a person we put on in our pasts and used to try to fit in with others. Now is the time to surround ourselves with a community of people who will speak life into us and fill us up rather than people who drain us because they only want to see the old version of us or the version they painted us out to be. It's time to take off the person we pretended to be to receive praise from others. It's time that we stop pretending simply to experience those fleeting feelings after moments of instant gratification. It's time to take off our masks and step away from the person others needed us to be that caused us to lose focus of our purposes and who God called us to be.

Will you have your identity credentials in Heaven, or will you have to tell God you bargained your identity on earth for accomplishments and lived as someone He did not call you to be?

PRAYER: God, help me to be myself. Help me be who You created me to be in this world so that I can fulfill the words of identity and destiny You have spoken over my life. Help me to walk in Your will so I can bring Your word back to You full. Amen.

Reflection

ACTION STEP: What are the words of identity and purpose God has spoken over your life? When it's time to bring God's word back to Him full and fulfilled, will you be able to say that you accomplished His word over your life?

Day 64
CORE VS. CROSS

*"If anyone asks what you are doing, just say,
'The Lord needs them,' and he will immediately let you take
them."*
Matthew 21:3 NLT

Passage of the Day: Matthew 21:1-11.

I believe God intended for the cross to be a symbol of love, sacrifice, and salvation. However, in today's society, the cross is simply seen as a fancy piece of jewelry and rarely an ideal way of life. Sadly, the cross and its symbolism have become something to wear but not something to pick up and carry. As believers, if we haven't already picked up our crosses, we should ask ourselves what is stopping us? Could it be that we need to change who we are at our cores?

Our cores represent our souls or the root of who we are as humans. We express who we are spiritually, mentally, emotionally, physically, and so much more from our cores. We live our lives from our cores, and as a result, we have to be careful and intentional about what we allow to enter our cores. If not, we may find ourselves producing and bearing fruit in our lives that is not Christlike. In addition, we have to cooperate with God and yield to the Holy Spirit, so God can remove anything from our cores that is not like Him. Prayer and fasting are also important as we continue to purify and develop who we are at our cores. Prayer and fasting allow us to take the necessary steps to remove anything preventing us from carrying our crosses.

Picking up your cross may not be the easiest thing to do, as it can potentially come with some opposition. Everyone will not understand your calling or the new person God is calling you to be because the call of God isn't a conference call. When we walk with the Lord, we can't run with the world. It's time to upgrade our cores, release the older version of ourselves, and pick up our crosses and walk.

PRAYER: God, help me to heal and upgrade who I am at my core, so I may go on and pick up my cross and walk into who You have called me to be. Amen.

Reflection

ACTION STEP: What is stopping you from picking up your cross? What can you do to move forward into who God called you to be and pick up your cross?

Day 65
FEEDING YOUR SPIRIT

"When I saw him, I fell at his feet as if I were dead. But he laid his right hand on me and said, "Don't be afraid! I am the First and the Last. I am the living one. I died, but look—I am alive forever and ever! And I hold the keys of death and the grave."
Revelation 1:17-18 NLT

Passage of the Day: Luke 24:13-35 and Revelation 1:17-18.

Have you ever received a word from God that didn't match how you felt?
For instance, maybe God is telling you, you're going to get a new job or heal from a relationship that has ended. However, as you wait in hopeful expectation for these blessings or miracles to happen, you begin to ask God why isn't anything changing. We can often become upset, frustrated, and doubtful in these moments, but are we expressing how we feel to God? It's important to communicate and release negative feelings or emotions to God because sometimes our feelings can turn into spirits. Those feelings of anger, bitterness, and doubt can turn into spirits we carry with us each day. And when our spirits are not in check, we can potentially become a stumbling block for others, causing them to fall further into sin or away from God.

Our spirits determine our postures and how we show up in the world. Therefore, we have to learn how to control and take care of our spirits properly. We do this by being completely honest with God about how we feel. We lift up our feelings and emotions to God so He can help us. In addition, before entering any room, let us decide what spirit we will have before we allow others and their spirits to determine our postures for us. Then decide, no matter what we encounter in that room, we will not change our posture or waver on our decision. Lastly, we can also manage our spirits by asking ourselves what we have been feeding our spirits. Are we spending time with God and His word? Are we surrounding ourselves with people who sustain or those who drain us? What pages are we following on social media, and how do they make us feel? What are we watching on television or listening to on the radio daily? Make sure you take care of your spirit and feed it what it needs to thrive.

PRAYER: God, teach me how to take care of my spirit properly. Help me take control of my spirit and address what is getting in the way of becoming more honest with You. In Jesus' name. Amen.

Reflection

ACTION STEP: Take inventory of what you are feeding your spirit. Make a list of all the people you surround yourself with, television shows you watch, the music you listen to, social media pages you follow, etc. Think to yourself, is this the proper diet for my spirit?

Day 66
GOD'S GRACE

"Three different times I begged the Lord to take it away.
Each time he said, "My grace is all you need.
My power works best in weakness."
So now I am glad to boast about my weaknesses,
so that the power of Christ can work through me."
2 Corinthians 12:8-9 NLT

Passage of the Day: 2 Corinthians 12:7-10.

We all have something that hurts or hinders us. That *thing* that we can't seem to shake or loose. In 2 Corinthians 12:7, Apostle Paul gives his thing a name —he calls it his thorn. Based on the referenced scripture, a thorn is a consistent weakness that significantly impacts our lives, to the point that we desperately ask God to take it away from us. But what do we do when God says He isn't going to remove the thorn because what we view as a weakness, He plans to use to help us?

Anything that happens in our lives, God allows it. I believe we give the devil too much credit for the negative things that happen in our lives. Is he responsible for some of the hurt or chaos we experience—absolutely! But the Bible also teaches us that God uses trials and tribulations for our development (see James 1:2-4). And what the devil tries to use to destroy us, God can take it, turn that thing around and bless us. The trials, tests, and thorns we face can help us see who we are. When you feel weak, remember you are strong due to God's Grace. His Grace is sufficient for every thorn and every weakness.

"That's why I take pleasure in my weaknesses, and in the insults, hardships, persecutions, and troubles that I suffer for Christ. For when I am weak, then I am strong."
2 Corinthians 12:10 NLT

PRAYER: God, thank You for using my weaknesses to develop me. And thank you for not allowing the devil to use them to destroy me. In Jesus' name. Amen.

Reflection

ACTION STEP: Make a list of the different areas of your life (i.e., relationships, financial habits, etc.). Where do you see a need for growth, and what can you do to grow in those areas? How can those perceived weaknesses be turned into strengths?

Day 67
GOD'S NO

*"Now to Him who is able to do exceedingly abundantly
above all that we ask or think, according to the power that
works in us."*
Ephesians 3:20 NKJV

Passage of the Day: Ephesians 3:20 and Jeremiah 29:11

Have you ever prayed for something over and over
again, just for it not to happen? For instance, passing
a test, getting a new job, moving into a new home, or getting
a new car. When we pray for blessings such as the ones
previously mentioned, and we don't receive them, we may
begin to question God's love and faithfulness towards us.
Especially when we believe we are ready or deserving of the
blessing. However, here's the thing —when God says no, we
are reminded He is in control. According to Jeremiah 29:11,
God has a plan for each of our lives, and He cannot bless us
as He always intended if He is always listening to us. When
God doesn't give us what we are asking for, we should
acknowledge and give thanks for what we already have and
the beautiful plan God has in place to prosper us.

It's okay to tell God what we want, but we also should trust
that He will always give us what we need. And more times
than not, we ask for what we want, but God has something
bigger and better in store for us. Remember, when God
closes one door, He opens another, and He'll even open
a window for us. The no we receive can also mean that God

is giving us more time to become the person He needs and wants us to be to receive our blessings.

_____

PRAYER: God, thank you for giving me what I need and not what I want. Amen.

Reflection

ACTION STEP: Today, I want you to try something new. Whatever you have been praying for that hasn't happened yet, thank God for saying wait or no. When God says no, He declares that what you have is what you need to get you to where He is trying to take you. Start doing your part to manifest what God has in store for you and thank Him in advance for the blessings that are on the way.

Day 68
SECURITY

"And we know that God causes everything to work together for the good of those who love God and are called according to his purpose for them."
Romans 8:28 NLT

Passage of the Day: Romans 8:28.

In troubling times, we find security in God. But it may not always feel secure in God, especially when we find ourselves constantly in prayer and don't receive an immediate response from God. Hold tight to your faith in these moments because God hears every prayer, and He is always working in the background. God is a Man of His Word, and what He said will happen —will happen! We may not see the answered prayers immediately, but God is working on who we are spiritually, mentally, emotionally, physically, and financially in preparation for the greater good.

————————

PRAYER: God, thank you that my blessings are never delayed but always on time according to Your will. Amen.

Reflection

ACTION STEP: Think and write down all the ways God has come through for you in the past. Rehearse and remind yourself of these blessings as you wait on future ones from God.

Day 69
GOD'S PROMISES

"The Spirit of the Lord is upon me, for he has anointed me to bring Good News to the poor.
He has sent me to proclaim that captives will be released, that the blind will see, that the oppressed will be set free, and that the time of the Lord's favor has come."
Luke 4:18-19 NLT

Passage of the Day: Luke 13:10-17 and Luke 4:18-19.

In moments of unanswered prayers, doubt, stress, or anxiety, we can become ungrateful and lose sight of the current blessings in our lives. We may find ourselves constantly focused on our current situations, not realizing God has promised us a greater future. There is nothing we can ask for that will be greater than the promises God has for us. Rather than allowing our current situation to have us down in the dumps or sad and depressed, let's learn to lean into gratitude. Even if your current situation is not the best, think back over your life, acknowledge how far you've come, and celebrate that you are not in the same place you were before. You are now standing in what you once prayed for, and that is something to be grateful for.

If you are having trouble thinking of blessings to be grateful for, here are a few reminders of what God has already promised us in His word: joy in the morning, a prepared table of blessings in the presence of our enemies, to be a friend that sticks closer than a brother, and the promise that He will never leave nor forsake us. God's got us, and He is always looking out for us.

Even when we don't ask for something, God provides it because He knows our needs before we need them and sees things we cannot. God desires to bless us in every way possible, and He will do just that.

PRAYER: God, thank You for all the times You said no. I trust and know that you have something greater in store for me. Lord, let me see what You have promised so that I can hold onto those promises and hope for the future. Above all, Lord, allow your will to be done in my life. In Jesus' name. Amen.

Reflection

ACTION STEP: Think about and write down all God has promised you.

Day 70
CONTROL AND TRUST

*"Then he turned to the woman and said to Simon,
"Look at this woman kneeling here. When I entered your
home, you didn't offer me water to wash the dust from my
feet, but she has washed them with her tears and wiped
them with her hair."*
Luke 7:44 NLT

Passage of the Day: Luke 7:36-50.

Let's imagine ourselves running in a race. But instead of this being a marathon or a triathlon —this is the race of our lives. As we are running in our lanes, imagine that we happen to take a glance at someone who appears to be running ahead of us. The runner we are glancing at has a house, a brand new car, designer clothes, and over fifty-thousand followers on Instagram. We keep running and shift our focus back to our race, but when compared to others, we now feel our lives do not amount to anything or have no real meaning. Slowly we begin to lose control of our stride, and we decide that the only way to keep up with the other runners is to abandon God and take control of our situations and lives. Moving forward, we choose to take shortcuts instead of following the path and timelines God has set for us. After doing our own thing and running outside of the will of God, we feel bold and in control. We look at the other runners and notice we are now in the lead —or so we think. Suddenly, we find ourselves running into many hurdles and obstacles and eventually back to where we originally started.

Control and trust go hand in hand, and to show we fully trust God, we must relinquish control of our lives over to Him. Can we honestly say we trust God if we are constantly disobeying His commands and moving ahead of Him in our lives? How will we receive the promises of God if we continue to take shortcuts to where He is trying to take us and continuously operate outside of His will for our lives. What God has in store for us is bigger and greater than any prize we can acquire on our own merit. And what God has for us is different than what He planned for those running next to us. Our blessings and promises are tailored made just for us. From this moment forward —surrender. Allow God's will to be done in your life and surrender yours.

PRAYER: God, help me relinquish control of my life over to you, and show me how to surrender to Your will for my life. In Jesus' name. Amen.

Reflection

ACTION STEP: What stops you from relinquishing control of your life over to God? What steps can you take to relinquish control?

Day 71
WHERE YOU ARE

"He had to go through Samaria on the way."
John 4:4 NLT

Passage of the Day: John 4:1-26.

Has there ever been a time in your life when you have felt lost in the world? Have you ever felt like you didn't have a purpose, or maybe you've felt overlooked, almost nameless to society? When our prayers go unanswered, we may even start to think God doesn't see us, remember us or know our names. Thoughts of confusion (e.g., *"What did I do to deserve this?"*) may even start to play in our minds.

I am here to remind you that God loves you, and He loves you exactly as you are. God sees you; He remembers you; He knows your name and everything about you. The Bible tells us that God has written our names on the palms of His hands (see Isaiah 49:16) and knows each of us so intimately that He knows the number of hairs on our heads (see Luke 12:7). God is always listening; He wants to hear from us, and He is not ignoring our prayers. When God hears our prayers and our cries for help, He often sends Jesus to meet us where we are. No matter where we are located, Jesus will show up for us and meet us there. And when Jesus steps into our place or times of need, He is not there to judge us. No matter our station in life or the mistakes we've made, Jesus loves us beyond our race, gender, sexual orientation, or sins. When we stand in need, God shows up to provide and meet those needs.

Whenever you find yourself in a moment where you feel empty and without purpose —wait on God. God will defy earthly standards and break every code of normalcy to help us and provide us with all we need. When Jesus arrives on the scene and meets us where we are, let's remember to welcome Him with open arms. Because our Heavenly Father is always patiently waiting for our return back to Him with open arms.

If you ever need a pick me up, try listening to "He Still Loves Me" by The Passionate Prophets.

PRAYER: Jesus, thank You for continuously meeting me where I am. Amen.

Reflection

ACTION STEP: Listen to "He Still Loves Me" by the Passionate Prophets. Journal your thoughts and revelations while listening to the song.

Day 72
ARE YOU LONELY?

*"And I will ask the Father,
and he will give you another Advocate,
who will never leave you."*
John 14:16 NLT

Passage of the Day: John 14:15-18 and 1 Kings 19:1-3, 9-10.

The spirit of loneliness is an oppressive spirit that makes us feel like we are alone in the world and forgotten by those around us. When we feel alone, every day feels like a mission we are fighting by ourselves. There are good days and bad days, and on both days, we feel like we are walking through life alone. On the good days when we can scream in victory, there is no one to celebrate with us. And on the bad days, there is nobody there to comfort us. When we feel alone or don't have any support, we also tend to isolate ourselves from others because we don't want to feel like a burden. We become accustomed to handling everything on our own and proudly wear the badge of sole survivor. However, solitude, isolation, and loneliness are not God's desires for any of His children. In Genesis 2:18, God clarifies that it is not good for man (meaning humanity) to be alone. In John 14:16, Jesus promised the Holy Spirit to all believers. And the gift of the Holy Spirit ensures we are never alone because He is always with us. The Holy Spirit lives within us. He is the voice inside of us, reminding us of God's love and teaching us right from wrong. When we are feeling down and need lifting up —The Holy Spirit is there to comfort us and remind us of every promise in God's word. He speaks to our dreams, passions, thoughts, and emotions. He is also our Ever-Present Help, Life's Tour Guide, Nurturing Comforter, and so much more!

Remember, we have the Holy Spirit within us whenever we feel lonely. Welcome Him into your heart. Instead of trying to survive in life, learn to thrive with the help of the Holy Spirit.

PRAYER: Holy Spirit, thank You for being ever-present in my life. Thank You for never leaving me alone. Thank you for always being with me. Amen.

Reflection

ACTION STEP: Think of all the ways the Holy Spirit has comforted you when you felt alone.

Day 73
BE STILL

"There is only one thing worth being concerned about.
Mary has discovered it, and it will not be taken away from her."
Luke 10:42 NLT

Passage of the Day: Luke 10:38-42 and Genesis 2:2-3

We live in a world where being still and resting in God is looked down upon and criticized. Does the phrase *"I'll sleep when I die"* sound familiar? We live in a society that teaches us to push ourselves beyond our limits. A world that teaches us to work hard to stay booked and busy, so people don't see us as lazy or unmotivated. Some of us even keep ourselves busy because we are running from ourselves. We can't sit or be still because that means we have to sit with our thoughts, histories, and traumas and deal with them.

Furthermore, some of us have many dreams and aspirations, and we fear if we take a break, it'll delay us in our journey. Sure, it is absolutely important to make good use of the time God has given us. However, we must ensure that we are using that time wisely. And using our time wisely includes being still, taking breaks, and spending time in the presence of God. sexual orientation, or sins. When we stand in need, God shows up to provide and meet those needs.

When we are constantly active and obsessively committed to the next project, accolade or goal, we tend to miss out onwhat God is trying to do in our lives now. But I'm here on an assignment from God to remind us all that it's okay to slow down, rest, and be still in the presence of God. To truly carry forth God's word on our lives and serve Him — we need to create intentional moments of recharge and rejuvenation. We need to plan intentional moments and space in our lives for rest. During those rest periods, we should also address the thoughts, unresolved emotions, and past experiences we've been avoiding. And proper rest will prepare us for the next leg of our race and journey.

PRAYER: God, help me to be still. Amen.

Reflection

ACTION STEP: Think about ways to be still and rest today.

Day 74
LOST AND FOUND

"And don't worry about those donkeys that were lost three days ago, for they have been found. And I am here to tell you that you and your family are the focus of all Israel's hopes."
1 Samuel 9:20 NLT

Passage of the Day: 1 Samuel 9:16-24 and Isaiah 43:18-19

Have you ever lost something that you so desperately wanted back? Something you would even risk your peace for because it was that important to you? Throughout my journey in life, I've learned God is in the business of giving us back what we thought we lost. God wants us to evolve and grow into the people He wants and needs us to be. For us to do that, sometimes God has to strip us of the things we love. But God is a Restorer and desires to give back or replace those things we had to give up. However, when God gives us back what we thought we lost, we cannot go back to the old version of ourselves. He wants us to show up as our full selves —our new selves —and steward the gift based on who we are now, not who we used to be.

As you journey through the various seasons of your life, trust God's sovereignty and stop looking for what was lost. God is always doing a new thing in our lives. For every blessing or relationship, we thought we lost, God has something greater awaiting us in the future. He has already gone ahead of us and begun to whisper to those people in our new places of elevation that we have what they are looking for, and we are coming. He even exposes us to our next level by allowing us to visit spaces and rooms we will soon occupy for good. God is working in the next dimension for our benefit. Let's not become so consumed with what was lost that we forget about the overflow that often comes from it. What God has in store for us is bigger and greater than anything we have lost!

PRAYER: God, thank you for giving me what I lost. Amen.

Reflection

ACTION STEP: Write down what God has given you back that you lost.

Day 75
GOD'S LOVE

" For I am convinced that neither death nor life, neither angels nor demons, neither the present nor the future, nor any powers, neither height nor depth, nor anything else in all creation, will be able to separate us from the love of God that is in Christ Jesus our Lord."
Romans 8:38-39 NIV

Passage of the Day: Romans 8:38-39 and Luke 15:1-12.

Have you ever doubted God's love for you?

Sometimes we think that God doesn't love us because of our sins, flaws, or mistakes. We allow shame and guilt to distance us from God because we fear that God will reject us due to the nature of our sins. I'm here to remind us all that nothing we do in life can separate us from the love of God. God does not stop loving us because of our shortcomings, and He is not keeping count of our sins, flaws, or mistakes. His love for us is infinite and lasts forever. In addition, God's love is not based on our earthly acquisitions or accolades. He doesn't care about how much money we have, the clothes we wear, or the level of fame we have ascended to in life. God judges who we are based on who we are in our hearts and loves us simply for who we are.

God created, loves, and cherishes each and every one of us. No matter how many times we may sin or stray away from Him, God's love for us remains, and He'll never give up on us.Through Him, we experience the true definition of a Father's love. If you've distanced yourself from God because of your mistakes in life, take some time to talk to God, turn back to Him, and develop a deeper relationship with Him.

Today, I encourage you to listen to 'Calling My Name' by Hezekiah Walker.

PRAYER: God, thank You for loving me for who I am.

Reflection

ACTION STEP: How can you take more time out of your day to get to know God more?

Day 76
REMAINING CALM

"The Lord himself will fight for you. Just stay calm."
Exodus 14:14 NLT

Passage of the Day: Nehemiah 8:9-12 and John 7:37-38.

When we relinquish control of our lives over to God and start to feel like God has forgotten us because nothing is happening in our lives —we can start to wrestle with thoughts of confusion and frustration. As a result, we may eventually move into a space where we take back control of our lives from God because things are not moving fast enough for us. We start operating from a place of *"I got it from here."* However, it's important to remember that our blessings are never delayed, and God is always on time. Behind the scenes, God is always fighting battles on our behalf. Things are changing spiritually in our lives before we see evident changes on the outside. God desires to set us up for success. Instead of falling into frustration, we should look for opportunities to prepare for the future success and fullness God is planning for us. The waiting season also builds and fortifies our trust in God.

Let's continue to relinquish control of our lives over to God. Great things are in store for us, and it may take a little longer than expected, but God's word always comes through. God has a plan for each of our lives, and God designed that plan to prosper us, not to harm us, and to give us hope and a great future (Jeremiah 29:11). God would not lead us this far to fail. It is time to disrupt our negative thinking, remain calm, hold tight to our hope and trust God.

PRAYER: God, thank You for being in control. Amen.

Reflection

ACTION STEP: How can you disrupt your negative thinking today?

Day 77
FREEDOM

*"For you have been called to live in freedom,
my brothers and sisters.
But don't use your freedom to satisfy your sinful nature.
Instead, use your freedom to serve one another in love."*
Galatians 5:13 NLT

Passage of the Day: Luke 4:16-19 and Mark 8:36.

God created the world for human beings to enjoy, and some of the blessings we experience on earth were intended to make us happy. Due to God's design, it can be pretty easy to fall into the trap of using worldly pleasures to satisfy our needs. But can the world offer us everything we need to live genuinely fulfilling lives? The simplest answer —no. Our earthly experiences allow us to enjoy fleeting moments of happiness, but they do not offer us sustainable joy and peace. To experience true joy and peace on earth, God must serve as the head and center of our lives. Remember that Jesus is the Way, the Truth, and the Life, and He opens the door that gives us access to having an amazing relationship with God. Through our relationship with God, He frees us and blesses us with what we need to thrive in this world. What God can do for us the world could never do or offer us! God is always the answer.

PRAYER: God, thank You for blessing me with all that I need to thrive and experience true peace and joy. Amen.

Reflection

ACTION STEP: Write down your needs, and examine them. Currently, are you looking to God to satisfy those needs or the world?

Day 78
PRAYER WORKS

"Then Jesus called for the children and said to the disciples,
"Let the children come to me. Don't stop them!
For the Kingdom of God belongs to those who are like these
children."
Luke 18:16 NLT

Passage of the Day: Luke 18:1 and Luke 18:16-23.

Prayer simply represents the moments we set aside each day to connect with God and have conversations with Him. However, some of us struggle with connecting with God in prayer because we don't know what to say. Or we may be too afraid to speak to Him due to a lack of a relationship with Him. During these moments of fear or reluctance, the first thing to remember is God always wants to hear from us because we are His children. And what good Father doesn't want to talk to and spend time with His children? Secondly, we must remember to come before God humbly in prayer. When we come to God with humble hearts and humbled spirits, we are more open to hearing what He has to say to us. In addition, a humbled posture allows us to discern God's will for our lives and then submit to His plan for our lives. Next, we should talk to God the same way we talk to our family and friends. And when we still don't know what to say or how to say it, the Holy Spirit will give us the words to say, and He makes sure God hears our hearts and what we are trying to communicate to Him. Lastly, I love to pray using the acronym P.R.A.Y. —that stands for *Praise, Repent, Ask, and Yield.*

Praise: Start your prayer with praise, and that means thanking God for who He is and what He's already done in our lives.

Repent: Next, repent for your sins. Repentance simply means apologizing for any wrong you've done, asking for forgiveness for those wrongs, and agreeing to stop doing the wrongful act. It's another way we get back on the right path with God and choose to be better and do better.

Ask: Now, make your requests known to God. Tell Him exactly what you need or want and be specific. Remember to pray for yourself and others. Furthermore, be sure to ask for things that glorify God and are consistent with His word.

Yield: Take time to sit in silence and allow God to speak to you. Remember, prayer is a conversation with God —we should talk during prayer and listen.

Prayer is simply a conversation between you and God. During this conversation, be sure to bring every question, comment, or concern to God's attention. And even when using the acronym P.R.A.Y., our prayers do not have to be scripted or rehearsed. Allow it to flow, and simply speak to God truthfully and honestly.

PRAYER: God, thank You for wanting to hear from me. I submit my will to Yours and welcome Your will with an open heart into my life. Amen.

Reflection

ACTION STEP: Using the acronym P.R.A.Y., write a short prayer for the day, and then pray it aloud.

Day 79
LIVING IN PURPOSE

"And he said unto them, How is it that ye sought me?
wist ye not that I must be about my Father's business?"
Luke 2:49 KJV

Passage of the Day: Luke 2:46-52 and Jeremiah 1:5.

We were born with a gift and a purpose, something inside us that we will use to help change the world. However, many of us believe otherwise because of the discouraging words others have spoken to us, or we were never taught that we were valuable and had something to offer to the world. If this describes you, I want you to remember that God said we are fearfully and wonderfully made (see Psalm 139:14), and before He formed us in our mothers' wombs, He knew and purposed us (see Jeremiah 1:5). Or maybe you've become distracted by watching someone else's walk in life and purpose. As a result, we can often fall off course and forget that we have unique gifts and talents. If this scenario describes you, I want you to remember that God is always waiting for us to turn back to Him so He can help us get back on course and the path, He has set for our lives.

In addition, we can't become too focused or worried about God's master plan for our lives because this posture can cause us to lose focus on who He wants us to be in the current moment. If you're constantly focused on the bigger picture instead of the little steps that get us there, ask God to give you a heart of contentment for where you are now.

Then ask God to help you understand what He is doing in your life now —ask Him to make you more obedient to what He is doing now rather than focusing on what is coming next. From this place of contentment and humility, we can take the steps we need to take to be more present in our day-to-day lives while also doing what God is calling us to do now. Remember, we have to become the people God needs and wants us to be before we can receive the blessings of our tomorrow.

I also want to leave you with this final word for the day: what is impossible with man is possible with God (Luke 1:37). Allow God to use you each day by committing to living out your purpose one day at a time. Even if you don't love where you are in life, stay committed to shedding your light amongst others —do it truthfully and authentically. Sharing your testimony today can plant a seed in someone else that gets them started on their journey of living out their purpose. And as you keep serving others day by day, you'll show God He can trust you with the larger audience He may call you to help tomorrow. Be about your Father's business and live in your purpose —today!

PRAYER: God, thank You for creating me to be fearfully and wonderfully made. Thank You for assigning a purpose to my life that I can start living out today. Show me how to serve the world today and prepare me for the work You will have me perform in the future. Amen.

Reflection

ACTION STEP: How can you be more about your Father's business? What steps can you take today to become more present in the now and not the next?

Day 80
SCHOOL OF LIFE

"Now there was a believer in Damascus named Ananias.
The Lord spoke to him in a vision, calling, "Ananias!"
"Yes, Lord!" he replied."
Acts of the Apostles 9:10 NLT

Passage of the Day: Acts 9:10 and Luke 10:38-42

You may think you're doing what God is instructing you to do because you're making it through storms and passing tests, but what if you're not being tested like you think? Sometimes, we look at our struggles and the negative occurrences happening in our lives, and we automatically assume we are dealing with another negative test or storm of life. However, what if the moment of testing is actually God teaching and maturing us? Aside from being God's children, we are also His students —His disciples. Let's consider the concept of traditional school for a moment. In school, we usually study multiple subjects at once. I think it's safe to say that we excelled in some subjects, and we may have struggled in other subject areas. Similar to instructional schools, when we are under God's instruction, we are also learning many different life lessons all at once. Those life lessons are intended to prepare us to step into what God calls us to do. As you may recall, we were also required to take tests within the school setting. And before we take a test, the teacher provides instruction so we can learn and study up on the test's content. In God's school of life, our instruction is presented in various ways, and so are our tests. However, we have to be sensitive in the spirit and sensitive to the voice of God, so we can understand what God is trying to teach us, instead of thinking it's just another storm we have to fight and overcome.

God is always teaching, instructing, and maturing His children. It's our responsibility to humble ourselves before God, learn from Him, study His word, obey His Word, and apply what we are learning from Him to our lives. When we do this, we'll see how much our lives can change when we take the time to sit at the feet of our greatest teacher!

PRAYER: God, humble me to see what You are teaching me. Amen.

Reflection

ACTION STEP: Think about what God could be teaching you at this moment that you may have considered a storm or test. What can you learn from this?

Day 81
TO GOD BE THE GLORY

"Jesus responded, "Didn't I tell you that you would see
God's glory if you believe?"
So they rolled the stone aside.
Then Jesus looked up to heaven and said,
"Father, thank you for hearing me. You always hear me,
but I said it out loud for the sake of all these people stand-
ing here, so that they will believe you sent me."
John 11:40-42 NLT

Passage of the Day: John 11:40-42.

Do you remember classroom show and tell days in elementary school? In case you are not familiar with this American tradition, let me explain. On show and tell day, each student had to bring an object of significance to school and make an oral presentation in front of their class. Each student would present the object to the class, and explain why it was meaningful and important to them. In life, God expects us to use our triumphs and testimonies in the same way by giving Him glory for our lives.

When we give God His glory, we are showing and telling others about the goodness of God and what He has done for us. We should go beyond thanking God privately, to thanking Him publicly so others will know and believe in His greatness and power. Remember, tests and trials produce testimonies, which are meant to be shared with others. By God's design, we come out on the other end of our trials and tribulations bigger and better than we were before.

But after God brings us out, how many of us take the time to give Him glory? Yes, we have played our part in getting through the test or trial, but we can't forget to acknowledge God for what He did to help us through and how He used it for our good.

As you celebrate your victories in life, don't forget that God deserves His glory. We can't just call on God when we need help, then forget Him when things get better. God wants us to live abundantly and whole, for our sakes and the sake of others. He is the same yesterday, today and tomorrow. What He did for us He can do for others, but how will they know if no one tells them? To better serve God and simultaneously be a blessing unto others —we must give God is glory.

PRAYER: God, I apologize for not giving You continuous glory and acknowledgment for the amazing things You have done in my life. Give me a renewed spirit of boldness and help me break my silence to share with the world all the great things You have done in my life. In Jesus' name. Amen.

Reflection

ACTION STEP: What is one thing you can do today to give God glory?

Day 82
LOVING & DISAGREEING

"We love each other because he loved us first."
1 John 4:19 NLT

Passage of the Day: Matthew 7:24-27.

Sometimes it can be quite difficult to love someone who has different values, morals or character traits when compared to our own. We may find ourselves getting into disagreements with others, and struggling to find a common or respectful ground. We may even label others as "crazy, difficult, annoying, or evil", because they think or behave differently than us. However, First John 4:19, teaches us to love others simply because God first loved us. This is a hard stance to take, but the first step in loving others we don't agree with — is giving them the benefit of the doubt. Giving someone the benefit of the doubt, can mean trusting that they mean well even when we don't agree with them and vice versa. Or it could also mean recognizing that they lack a certain level of knowledge to understand our stance on a particular topic. Instead of bashing or criticizing them, we could take the stance of compassion and educate them. When we give others the benefit of the doubt, we eliminate our expectations of them and look beyond the way they are reacting to us. We may even start to ask ourselves questions like, *"What is causing them to act this way?"* We then lean into empathy, instead of judgement or anger. Furthermore, when we lean into empathy, we focus on becoming more understanding of that person. The need for being right is eliminated, we began to actively listen to them and we may find a place of common ground.

Sometimes that common ground looks like agreeing to disagree and loving one another anyway. This posture of love and compassion is easier said than done, but remember, when people see us, they should see and encounter the love of Christ. Instead of matching energy, keep your Christlike energy and shed your light. It'll make a difference in their life but most importantly, yours.

PRAYER: God, help me to love others the way in which You love me. Amen.

Reflection

ACTION STEP: How can you be more empathetic towards others, today?

Day 83
STUBBORNESS

"Jesus responded, "It isn't right to take food from the children and throw it to the dogs."
Matthew 15:26 NLT

Passage of the Day: Matthew 15:21-28.

L exico.com defines stubbornness as *"showing deter-mination not to change one's attitude or position on something."* Take a moment to think about the times in your life, past or present, when you were stubborn or adamant about a particular stance, or held a strong belief on a topic. Now, take a moment to ask yourself, do you hold the same level of passion and stubborn determination when it comes to your faith in God?

Life presents us with many ups and downs, and sometimes the downs of life can cause us to waver in our faith. But why is that? Why are we stubborn about so many other areas of our lives, but fold when it comes to our faith and trust in God? If all believers decided that we would be unyielding in our faith in God, we would experience less worry and anx-iousness about tomorrow. Because we would trust and know who holds tomorrow in His hands. In addition, we wouldn't focus so much on our weaknesses because we would hold on to the belief that God covers our weaknesses while giving us the ability to work beyond them. We would trust that He hears our prayers, and any delays were simply the result of Him taking His time to shape and mold us into the people He wants and needs us to be to carry out His word. We would trust that God wants the best for us, and trust that His delays are not denials.

Today, I want us to replace the negative connotation associated with the character trait of stubbornness. Then I want us all to embrace the trait and apply it to our faith. Stand ten toes down —unyielding —believing in God and His Word.

PRAYER: God, help me to fully embrace the character trait of stubbornness and then help me to become more stubborn when it comes to my faith in You and Your Word. In Jesus' name. Amen

Reflection

ACTION STEP: In what ways are you stubborn? How can you apply the character trait of stubbornness to your faith in God and His Word?

Day 84
INCONVENIENCE

"Later, when the boy was older, his mother brought him back
to Pharaoh's daughter, who adopted him as her own son.
The princess named him Moses, for she explained,
"I lifted him out of the water."
Exodus 2:10 NLT

Passage of the Day: Exodus 2:7-10.

Has something ever been such an inconvenience for you that you didn't want to do it anymore? Sometimes, God ordained purpose can feel like an inconvenience, especially depending on where we are in life. The inconvenience or pressures of purpose can feel overwhelming, and may even cause us to slow down or completely give up on purpose. However, I want to encourage us to resist stagnation and confront the inconvenience head on. To confront the inconvenience, we have to remember the significance and power of fulfilling our purpose. Our purposes help others by setting them free from their spiritual, mental, physical or emotional limitations. It also points others back to God when we share our stories and give God His glory. In addition, when we operate in God ordained purpose, we have the power to break generational curses, while making room and laying a strong foundation for the future generations of our families.

Our obedience to God should overrule any inconvenience we may encounter in our lives. Our purpose in life is bigger than us, and we should always keep that at the forefront of our minds.

Purpose stretches us, and it's one the reasons we will need to lean on God the most. When we come to God with our weaknesses and burdens, He always make a way. He provides us with the much needed tools and knowledge we need to thrive in purpose and overcome the hardships that comes along with it. Whatever inconveniences are present in your life, don't be afraid to confront them and face them head on, and be sure to ask for a helping hand from your Heavenly Father.

PRAYER: God, help me to confront inconvenience and become obedient to what You need me to do. Amen

Reflection

ACTION STEP: What is currently an inconvenience to you? How can you confront it?

Day 85
GUILT

*"But if we confess our sins to Him, He is faithful and just
to forgive us our sins
and to cleanse us from all wickedness"
1 John 1:9 NLT*

Passage of the Day: 1 John 1:9 NLT

Have you ever felt so guilty about a mistake you made or a sin you committed, that you distanced yourself from God? In the past, I have distanced myself from God because of mistakes I made, and I now realize my actions and response were rooted in fear. I feared that God would be so upset with me, and as a result, He wouldn't forgive me, and ultimately reject me. Instead of waiting for God to turn away from me, I turned away from Him first. It was like the more room I made for guilt and shame in my life, the less room I had for God. However, I came to realize that God loves us unconditionally and never gives up on us. God loves us so much that He sent His one and only Son to the cross to die for our sins and mistakes. God's grace and mercy covers our sins, and even when we make mistakes He never abandons or stops loving us.

Guilt often results from us placing our focus on ourselves. Whereas, the grace of God and the gratitude it produces in our hearts pushes our focus back to God. Instead of obsessing over ourselves and our mistakes, we should obsess over God's love and His grace. The heart of the Father is one of reconciliation, and He is always seeking relationship with us. Let today be the last day that we allow our feelings of guilt or shame to separate us from the Father's love.

PRAYER: God, thank You for loving me through and beyond my mistakes. Amen

Reflection

ACTION STEP: What are you currently feeling guilty about that is causing you to distance yourself from God? What do you need to do to reconcile yourself back to the Father?

Day 86
MARATHON

"As Jesus was walking along, he saw a man named Matthew sitting at his tax collector's booth. "Follow me and be my disciple," Jesus said to him.
So Matthew got up and followed him."
Matthew 9:9 NLT

Passage of the Day: Matthew 9:9 and Hebrews 12:1-2.

Life can be seen as an on-going race, or marathon. Throughput the journey we will encounter some sharp turns and hurdles, but we should not allow those circumstances to get in the way of us finishing our race. God deposited a purpose inside of each of us and He desires for us to fulfill that purpose during our time here on earth. He also dropped a word of destiny inside of each of us, and He expects us to bring it back to Him full. Purpose and destiny require us to pay close attention to what God is showing and telling us, so we can run our races with clarity and full determination. Growing up, my grandmother would often say, *"an idle mind can serve as the devil's playground"*. Her words taught me to stay focused on God, and the plans He set for my life. Her words also taught me not to get distracted by what's going on around me because everyone is running a different race.

God has a predestined plan for each of our lives and He did not create us to live stagnant, unfruitful or purposeless lives. It is time to get rid of our dead weight, stand tall and continue to push through to our finish lines. No matter how many times we've felt like giving up in the past, God did not give up on us and He won't give up on us now. This race we are running is not a sprint, it is more of a marathon which requires us to pace ourselves. Endurance, patience and divine victory will help us win this race. And remember, God is standing at the finish line —calling our names and rooting for us to win.

I also want to leave you with this final word for the day: We often pray for divine strength to make it through the race day by day. Today, let's think of ways we can utilize the strength God has already given us. Practicing self-care is one of the ways we harness the internal strength God has given us. Taking breaks for self-care also improves our endurance and stamina along the way. What can you do today to pour back into your strength tank?

PRAYER: God, thank You for never giving up on me, and blessing me with everything I need to run this race. Amen.

Reflection

ACTION STEP: Think of 3-5 ways (each) you can take care of yourself spiritually, mentally, emotionally, and physically.

Day 87
SERVING GOD

"Teach these new disciples to obey all the commands I have given you. And be sure of this: I am with you always, even to the end of the age."
Matthew 28:20 NLT

Passage of the Day: Matthew 28:16-20.

Question of the Day: When was the last time you prayed and asked God to show you how you can better serve Him through your life and actions?

During our prayer times with God, we often focus on asking God to help us. We rarely ask God to show us how we can help Him. Aside from being children of God, we are also students and servants of God. And our positions as students and servants require us to look for ways to serve Him. Our commitment to God should also include a commitment to completing the assignments He gives us, and blessing others. Nevertheless, at times, it is difficult to put our wants and needs aside to help others. It's especially hard when we are not in the best place in our own lives. However, having the posture or heart of a servant far outweighs the sacrifice of it. When we serve God, we align with His will, thoughts and desires —and blessings flow out of this place of alignment. Furthermore, the problems we are dealing with in our own lives are often handled when we simply focus on serving God.

I want to encourage us all to wake up each day and ask God, *"How can I serve you today?"* I believe this heart posture will unlock the blessings of God in our lives, while simultaneously allowing us to be a blessing unto others.

PRAYER: God, show me how can I better serve You today? Amen.

Reflection

ACTION STEP: In what ways can you serve the Lord today?

Day 88
TEMPTATION

"Where he was tempted by the devil for forty days.
Jesus ate nothing all that time and became very hungry."
Luke 4:2 NLT

Passage of the Day: Luke 4:1-13.

Have you ever finished eating a meal, but it wasn't as satisfying as you anticipated and you were left hungry for more? Maybe you were left hungry for something better, different or more gratifying. The same can be said about our everyday lives. The question I want us all to answer today — are you hungry for more?

When we see others pass a level we have been struggling with and witness how happy they appear to be, we may begin to hunger for instant gratification or a "right now" blessing. This hunger for the promises and blessings of God can often cause us to steer off course. However, we have to remember that we cannot take a shortcut to God's blessings. If we want to receive the blessings we've been praying for, we have to put in the work. It may not be easy but it will sure be worth it. Furthermore, we shouldn't envy or covet the blessings of others because we don't know what they had to go through or sacrifice in order to receive their blessings. If you need any more inspiration, the passage of the day details how Jesus fought the devil's temptations in the wilderness. We are capable of doing the same in our wilderness seasons. We have the power to fight temptation, we just have to use it. Let's dive into the word of God and strengthen our spirits.

God will guide us and bless us with all we need to overcome.

Take a moment to think about all the trials you have overcame. In every season of our lives, we are living in something we once prayed for. The problem is —we sometimes forget how far we've come and how much God has done for us. We also forget whose we are and Who we serve. The same God who blessed our neighbors, *will* bless us.

PRAYER: God, You are more than enough, and I don't need to hunger for more. Teach me how to live from a place of contentment and trust. Amen.

Reflection

ACTION STEP: Are you hungry for more? If so, what is causing you to hunger for more, and are your hungers causing you to drift further away from God's will for your life?

Day 89
YIELD

"Still other seed fell on fertile soil.
This seed grew and produced a crop that was a hundred
times as much as had been planted!"
When he had said this, he called out,
"Anyone with ears to hear should listen and understand."
Luke 8:8 NLT

Passage of the Day: Luke 8:4-15.

God dropped a word of destiny inside of each of us that we are supposed to bring back to Him full. But will the ground of your life yield to the word of God spoken over your life? Yes, God spoke a word of destiny and purpose over our lives, but will the ground of our lives prove to be good soil? Will the ground of our lives produce a ten-fold harvest that will testify to the glory of God? Have you heard the saying *"You reap what you sow?"* With this saying in mind, I want us to ponder on this question for a moment—*What have you sown lately?* Have you sown into purpose lately? Have you sown into destiny?

Isaiah 55:11 teaches us that when God speaks and declares a thing, His word cannot return to Him void. This simply means that when God says something it will surely come to pass. But we also have a part to play and a responsibility we must carry forth in order to ensure God's word over our lives is fulfilled. This responsibility requires us to show up in the world as our full selves, put in the work God is requiring us to complete, and take responsibility for what God needs and wants us to do. Yes, we love Jesus, but do we love Him enough to obey His word and submit our entire lives to His will for our lives. Yes, Jesus is our Savior but are we allowing Him to be Lord over our lives?

Today, say less in your prayers and allow God to say more. Ask God to show you how you can fully yield to Him and His word over your life. In addition, ask God to show you what He is waiting for you to do that you haven't done.

"So let's not get tired of doing what is good. At just the right time we will reap a harvest of blessing if we don't give up." Galatians 6:9 NLT

PRAYER: Heavenly Father, be a lamp unto my feet and show the steps I need to take to bring Your word back to You full. In Jesus's name. Amen.

Reflection

ACTION STEP: What has God been asking you to sow into that you are neglecting?

Day 90
DON'T WORRY

"Then, turning to his disciples, Jesus said,
"That is why I tell you not to worry about everyday life—
whether you have enough food to eat or enough clothes to wear.
For life is more than food, and your body more than clothing."
Luke 12:22-23 NLT

Passage of the Day: Luke 12:13-25 and Luke 12:31.

God is our one and only Source, but we sometimes fall into the trap of putting resources before God. Resources can include finances, clothing, cars or even social media —just to name a few. The absence or presence of these resources can also have an ungodly control over us, and when we put resources before God it can lead us down the wrong path. A hunger and love for earthly resources can lead us down paths of greed, compromise, envy, and pride. Sometimes, more earthly blessings or worldly acquisitions can also cause some people to drift further away from God. To avoid this trap, it is important to remember to we should put all our faith in God, not our earthly possessions. We can't become so focused on temporary things that we let what is enteral slip away.

The Bible teaches us not to worry about everyday life or the things of this world. Luke 12:31 reminds us to seek first God's kingdom, and He will give us everything we need — including the desires of our hearts. Remember success here on earth means nothing if God is not a part of it (see Psalm 127:1).

PRAYER: God, thank You for being my one and only Source! Amen.

Reflection

ACTION STEP: List any resources you may be putting before God or us.

About the Author

John C. Fuller is a Social Worker, Mental Health Therapist, and most importantly, a Man of God from Elizabeth, New Jersey. He received his Bachelor of Arts in Justice Studies from Montclair State University and his Masters in Social Work from Rutgers University.

John currently resides in the DMV area, where he is actively working as a school social worker in Southeast DC. He is licensed to provide mental health services in the states of Washington DC and Maryland. As a licensed therapist, John helps his students and clients discover and utilize their strengths to develop healthy lifestyles while also helping his clients rediscover their internal voices. John believes we all have a purpose in life and sees himself as a purpose agent assisting others in finding the confidence they need to walk in their God-ordained purpose.

Through his literary work, John hopes to take the timeless truths found in the Bible and translate them into a language that believers and non-believers alike can understand. John wants to help others connect more with God and, as a result of a deeper connection —walk fully into the plans and purposes God has destined for their lives according to Jeremiah 29:11. God's plans for each of us are good, and John wants to ensure we all experience that goodness.

"God wants us to live our best lives, but for us to do that, we must align with God's will for our lives and walk in the divine purpose He has assigned to our lives.
God gave each of us a job to complete while we are here, and we must develop as individuals to stand successfully in the position that God reserved for us."

– John C. Fuller

Connect with John

Official Website: johncfuller.com
Email: johncfuller93@gmail.com
Instagram: @Fullerr
Twitter: @AWordForUs_

nformation can be obtained
Gtesting.com
USA
940522
0038B/1154